W9-DCC-417

BIOREGIONAL PLANNING

For Toby, Ben and Fiona
and the next 40 generations

BIOREGIONAL PLANNING

Resource Management Beyond the New Millennium

David J. Brunckhorst
Department of Ecosystem Management
and
UNESCO Institute for Bioregional Resource Management
University of New England, Armidale, Australia

London and New York

Transferred to Digital Printing 2002
by Routledge, 11 New Fetter Lane, London EC4P 4EE

Routledge is an imprint of the Taylor & Francis Group

British Library Cataloguing in Publication Data

A catalogue record for this book is available from the British Library.

ISBN 90-5823-046-5

Cover design by *Epito Design*.

Printed and bound in Great Britain by TJI Digital, Padstow, Cornwall

TABLE OF CONTENTS

PREFACE

In the history of the biosphere of planet earth, a millennium is but a moment. In much less than a thousand years humanity has brought the biosphere—the giver of products essential for life, living space, quality-of-life, variety-of-life and national economies—to crisis point. The biosphere is now giving us many signals that it is greatly stressed; that it is struggling to cope with natural resource depletion, ozone depletion, acid rain, ecosystem loss, polluted air, land, rivers and oceans. Yet our future depends on it.

Much has been written about the traumas facing the Earth. There has been loss of biodiversity, not just genes and species, but of ecosystems and functional processes necessary to support healthy living communities including human ones—social systems relying on productive agriculture, goods, services and trade. The large spatial (and temporal), even global, scale of these interrelated and synergistic ailments are also beginning to be understood, or at least recognised.

Less has been written on the strategic actions necessary to plan for, manage and adapt to Ecologically Sustainable Development another thousand years into the future—beyond the new millennium. If humanity along with the rest of biodiversity in the biosphere is to have a sustainable future and reasonable quality of life, we need to start thinking and experimenting with comparably large-scale planning and (adaptive) management of human natural resource use and replenishment. Bioregional applications focus on landscape or regional scales of land-use planning and management. However, bioregions are not viewed in this book as purely ecologically defined regions. To be used as well as useful in a management context they must also reflect human identity with the local regional landscapes, a sense of place, in addition to ecological processes operating across those landscapes. Essentially these are cultural landscapes or biocultural regions defined, importantly, by ecological and biophysical features but also by the (human) communities, social systems and political economies within (or affecting) them.

This book focuses on the practical development and application of a bioregional approach to planning and managing for a sustainable future. It endeavours to provide a balanced pragmatic mixture of science, landscape ecology, ecosystem management, sociology, policy development and methods for transforming social and institutional cultures. It attempts to draw together and integrate requirements for sustainable conservation with sustainable development, sustainable natural resource use and production, with other needs such as ecologically restorative industries, economies, and social rehabilitation. I hope it might be of use well beyond the new millennium and beyond jurisdictional divides for any country or society pursuing a sustainable future.

David Brunckhorst
August 1999

ACKNOWLEDGMENTS

I greatly appreciate the interest and support of the Environment Department of the Australian Federal Government, which provided funding and is boldly attempting to work towards bioregional management and planning in partnership with State and local governments and local communities. UNESCO, UNEP, the IUCN, International Development programs, the World Bank and several Canadian and United States agencies are also moving to reshape their programs toward bioregional or ecoregional planning and implementation with communities. Manuscript preparation was assisted by a grant from Environment Australia and visiting fellowship to the Australian National University, Centre for UNESCO Visiting Fellows.

The development of this book owes an enormous debt to many friends, colleagues, reviewers who have at various times provided information, advice and encouragement, stimulating discussions, critique or comment. These kind people include: Andrew Beattie, Peter Bridgewater, Phil Coop, Ian Cresswell, Terry DeLacy, Tony Lynch, John Langmore, Errol Meidinger, David Mouat, Jim Omernik, Pam Parker, Bob Pressey, Nick Reid, Bill Rutherford, Nick Rollings, Mike Scott, Margaret Shannon, Simon Smith, Margaret Herring, Richard Thackway, Hank Tyler and Ian Reeve. Thanks also to Les and Debbie of *Epito Design* for the cover artwork.

All opinions expressed in the book along with any errors or omissions remain my responsibility and do not in any way reflect the policies of the above organisations or individuals.

To all my family, especially Shireen, go huge thanks for your perseverance and support. My sincere wish for our children and the next 40 generations is for a healthy and sustainable social and environmental future—way beyond the new millennium.

CHAPTER 1

INTRODUCTION: A SUSTAINABLE FUTURE BEYOND THE NEW MILLENNIUM?

Each generation has its own rendezvous with the land, for despite our fee titles and claims of ownership, we are all brief tenants on this planet. By choice or by default, we will carve a land legacy for our heirs.

Stewart L. Udall, 1988

Try to imagine in your mind a landscape that has not changed for a thousand years. There is no net movement of animals or plants. Neither the cycle of the seasons, nor death and renewal occurs. Life is stagnant because growth does not occur, biomass does not change. Nothing changes in space or time across this imaginary landscape. Clearly this is not possible, as no landscape remains unchanged. Ecological processes, evolutionary mechanisms and geological forces are continually reshaping landscapes across various scales of time and space, even within what we know of as wilderness. In the history of the biosphere, a millennium is but the twinkling of an eye. Amidst natural change over the last millennium, the effects of human activity have become increasingly felt, and now reach to the outermost atmosphere of planet earth – far more remote to that which we classify as wilderness. Our future, along with the rest of life on earth, depends on landscapes that can support ecological functional processes. To survive beyond the next millennium, human culture depends on the services provided by fully functioning ecological systems. The challenge into and beyond the next millennium is to halt the biosphere degrading effects of human society across several scales of space and time for a more enduring and harmonious relationship with natural processes.

Yet, the earth's resources are diminishing and nature is in retreat. In less than a century, human population and its requirements for space, materials, goods, and amenities have increased by more than five-fold (Ehrlich 1995). Over the past sixty years alone, the explosive growth rates of the global human population and our insatiable consumption of resources have been the cause of widespread collapse of the natural ecosystems. The production of human food and fibre has resulted in the wholesale simplification of many ecosystems and over utilisation of the natural capital resource base. The litany of examples are well-known: the over-harvest of forests, draining of wetlands, spread of agricultural development and high rates of pesticide and fertiliser use, the spread of feral pests, excessive clearing of woodland for domestic stock, urbanisation of foreshores, and the pollution of rivers and estuaries.

Regrettably many species have been lost. Arguably far more serious are the growing signs of functional problems in the operation of many ecological systems (Hobbs 1993, Naeem *et al*, 1994). Blue-green bacterial blooms in rivers and lakes are symptoms of breakdown of ecosystem processes and function. Even more disturbing because they are unseen by most people, are signs of biosphere dysfunction such as the expanding hole in the ozone layer, global climate change and acid rain (Hempel 1996). Ecosystem function, which individual species alone cannot perform, is of primary importance in sustaining the entire biosphere.

BIOSPHERE ECONOMICS

The biosphere is that part of the earth that supports life - providing our living space and our economy. Natural productivity and biodiversity are the warehouses for replenishing and supporting our global society. In this way, the human economy is a component of human society, which is in turn part of the biosphere (Figure 1.1). Unfortunately, too often the biosphere is relegated to a small concern of society, which sees itself as a cog in the larger system of modern economy. This economic rationale is the dominant model for decision making in most countries today. It proposes that the biosphere can be looked after best when the economy is functioning well. The opposite model, required for an ecologically sustainable future, suggests that the economy can be looked after best when the biosphere is functioning well.

Modern economies are shaped partly by natural factors that give developed nations an apparent advantage in the economic short-term in various activities - yet arguably a long-term disadvantage. Using economic rationale, policy decisions encourage those activities in an attempt to maintain their competitiveness in the face of market forces. Abundant freshwater would certainly appear to be a natural advantage, necessary for drinking, agriculture, and industry. Yet when governments set water pricing below the real cost of supply for, say, irrigation, taxpayers provide a subsidy for agricultural water use, encouraging overuse and fouling. This happens in Australia, the United States, South Africa and European countries. In contrast, government (or local community) policies based on the model that first considers biosphere functional capacity would promote a sustainable clean water supply over reckless economic rationalism (Figure 1.1). Melbourne, Australia, has one of the cleanest water supplies of any city on the globe today because the visionary forefathers totally protected vast areas of native forest catchment, and buffer areas around catchments for the population and development they could hardly imagine 200 years further on. They put a very high value on long-term, continuing supplies of clean water.

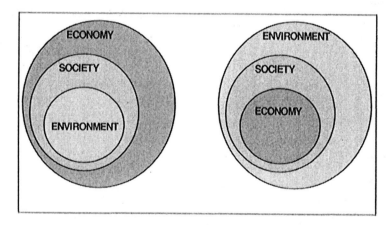

Figure 1.1. Economic rationale (Left) is the dominant model for decision making in most countries. It proposes that the environment can be looked after best when the economy is good. The model required for an ecologically supportable future views the economy as a component of human society, which is in turn part of the ecological systems of the entire biosphere (Right).

Maintaining Ecological Security

The maintenance of ecological processes across large areas of land and sea is crucial to climatic and water cycles, soil production, nutrient storage and pollutant breakdown (see Daily 1997). The diversity of plant and animal species now available to us relies on these ecological processes. We need to keep in mind that, all the world's food and many of our medicines and raw materials are derived from this biological diversity and continuing ecological processes. While we utilise only a tiny proportion of ecological diversity available to us, there is likely to be great scope for as yet unused genetic stock to offer new varieties, or improvements in currently commercialised species. For example, Australia has 15 of the earth's 16 known species of wild soybean and these could be of direct value in the future by providing disease-resistant or other genetically diversified stock.

In addition to physical needs, accessible, untrampled natural environments are also essential to the spiritual well being of humankind. Some sense of harmony with the natural world is a requirement for psychological and spiritual health as well as being a source of immeasurable aesthetic pleasure. Everyone needs the opportunity to enjoy the peace and beauty of nature. Human beings are ecologically interdependent with the natural world, just as other species are with each other.

Public reaction against the loss of biodiversity and loss of productivity from natural systems is growing. The ratification of the *Convention on Biological Diversity* gives authority and momentum to the campaign to maintain ecological security. Citizens are increasingly concerned with clean air, water and non-toxic food products, as well as protecting a greater proportion of the environment and species assemblages parks and reserves. Many countries are now actively exploring ways to build better reserve networks that comprehensively represent biological diversity and protect natural heritage. However most existing or new reserves will contribute little to sustaining the arguably more important ecological processes and functions at landscape and seascape scales that are fundamental to the health of all life. Even if effectively managed, these protected areas can only ever conserve a very small portion of the world's biodiversity. Yet the erosion of ecological systems and processes continues. Reserves and other protected areas are a necessary, but quite insufficient means alone to maintain biodiversity and ecological processes and functions that humans require for producing food, goods and services as well as other quality-of-life values. We rely on healthy functioning landscape ecosystems for our own health, longevity, security and well being.

No species, no matter how dominant, is independent of all the others. The existence of each depends to some extent on the existence of all. Humanity needs to learn to live within ecological laws that govern the capacity of the biosphere. Ecological law embodies the rules and conditions for nature's services, ecosystem processes and biosphere function across all scales in order to maintain a healthy productive environment. To secure our own future, one of the fundamental goals of society and economics should be to ensure the survival of all forms of life processes within the biosphere

(Figure 1.1). Preserving the roles of assemblages of species in ecosystems and their ability to continue to adapt or change (i.e. evolve) through time, is vital to sustaining biodiversity and ecosystem processes (Hansen and di Castri 1992). The diversity of the biosphere has provided the fundamental building blocks for tens of thousands of years of human food, shelter and culture (Wilson 1992). Now, as ever, it underpins ecologically sustainable development for current and future generations.

Those aware of the complexity of biodiversity understand that global interdependence is a necessary part of ecological security. Maintenance of biodiversity in one country depends in part on maintenance of biodiversity in others. That is one reason for the importance of the international *Convention on Biodiversity*, and the strategies that have emanated from it (eg, *Agenda 21, Local Agenda 21*). We have a responsibility to each other and our descendants to ensure ecological security now and in the future. The three basic requirements for an ecologically supportable future depend therefore on sustaining ecological integrity, natural capital and biodiversity (Box 1.1).

Box 1.1. Three ecological requirements for a sustainable future for the biosphere

ECOLOGICAL INTEGRITY   The health and resilience of natural life-support systems, including their capacity to assimilate wastes and endure pressures such as climate change and ozone depletion.

NATURAL CAPITAL   Sustaining the store of renewable natural resources - eg, productive soil, fresh water, forests, clean air, ocean - that underpin the survival, health and prosperity of human society.

BIODIVERSITY   Maintaining the variety of genes, species, populations, habitats and ecosystems.

Integrating Social Issues

Just as important as the ecological requirements listed above, novel approaches are needed to integrate societal values and the requirements for an ecologically supportable future. The impetus for developing and implementing such a sustainable systems approach on a landscape or regional basis is now coming from many directions, including economic, ecological and social studies (eg, Kim and Weaver 1994, Noss and Cooperrider 1994, Brunckhorst 1995, Brunckhorst and Bridgewater 1995, Gunderson et al. 1995, Steinitz et al. 1996, Costanza and Folke 1997, Berkes and Folke 1998). In essence, these studies have observed failures in current policy and management to produce practical information for decision making and planning that meets social and economic needs while conserving and respecting the limits of biophysical resources (Brunckhorst 1998). Many of these failures relate more to social institutions and management problems than to our lack of knowledge about ecosystems and human effects on them. Such management problems include, for example, too much reliance upon 'top-down' approaches, economic determinism, institutional and cross-jurisdictional competition, and poor application of existing information.

Governments attempt to balance the equitable distribution of finite resources across multiple and competing sectoral interests. However, in practice, they do not have all the funds required to implement the variety of programs and on-ground action to meet the challenges of environmental deterioration, biodiversity protection and sustainable resource use. Difficulties in mobilising resources for environmental action are often the consequence of the economic rationale model described earlier. For example, the goal of many modern governments is toward continued economic growth that would seem to undermine moves towards an economically and ecologically sustainable society. An alternative future for an ecologically sustainable society would require social transformations towards a more restorative economy where investment in biodiversity protection and environmental restoration provides, among many benefits, the 'growth capital' for future sustainable industries (Hawken 1993, Brunckhorst et al. 1997).

There are signs for optimism however, as the situation in several industrialised countries is very similar to that described by Roger DiSilvestro (1993) for the United States:

> Fortunately, survey after survey during the past decade has shown that citizens are willing to pay higher taxes or higher prices for material goods if, in return, they receive a cleaner, healthier, ecologically more stable environment. Many politicians have failed to keep up with the times and have

stood as obstacles to growing environmental concern. Politicians who remain
dreadfully out of touch with the will of their own nation seal their own fate.

Roger DiSilvestro (1993: 243)

Social and institutional transformations are required. If society has expectations that are inconsistent with human connections in the biosphere, then new technology and mounting masses of biological data will be ineffective in halting ecological destruction. The basic challenges have been clear for some time, yet most research has focused too much on classic reductionist studies with little application or transfer to natural resource management dilemmas (Lovejoy 1995, Brussard 1995). There is still too little understanding of the relationship between society and ecosystems at the scale of biocultural landscapes, which I refer to as bioregions. It is not the small-scale self-sufficient communities advocated by some "deep ecologists" (eg, Sale 1985).

BIOREGIONAL PLANNING FOR A SUSTAINABLE FUTURE

Environmental planning and management is a growing field, spending billions of dollars internationally to confront some of the most compelling problems faced by modern society. Until recently these problems were broken up into small parts under the jurisdiction of individual agencies and local governments. The failure of individual sectors to solve large environmental problems has led, in recent years, to an increasing interest in collaborative, multi-disciplinary approaches to landscape scale design, planning and management (see McHaug 1969, Tillman 1985).

Several impediments limit the holistic application of cultural and environmental understanding to integrated environmental planning and natural resource management. These include obstacles to integration not only of a narrow view and application of natural resource management, but also impediments to holistic approaches to watershed or catchment management, wildlife management, community-based programs, land/sea management and resource use, and ecologically sustainable development. A strictly defined, purely biophysical classification is unlikely to provide a practical implementation framework integrating nature and society. In fact it is very difficult to define human management units within such a framework. In, addition, the connectivity of nature (including human activity) across adjacent and even more distant ecosystems is increasingly being recognised. The successful integration of these issues will generally be at the scale of *across* related ecosystems, at a minimum. This is the operational scale of regional biocultural landscapes for social organisation fitting the landscape scale of linked ecological processes and services – the Bioregional Framework described here.

The concept of a *bioregion* as used in this book refers to a regional-landscape scale of matching social and ecological functions as a unit of governance for future sustainability that can be flexible and congruent still with various forms of government found around the world. This book discusses bioregion approaches as integrative planning and management tools also nesting with various elements of society or resource use, but integrating horizontally across the restrictive and disruptively fragmented jurisdictions. In acknowledging humans as a part of landscape-scale ecosystems, bioregions provide a pragmatic holistic management context based on both human culture and environmental attributes.

Generational sustainability also requires long-term vision and social flexibility (Smil 1993). It needs strategic integrated planning, policy development and implementation across traditional jurisdictional boundaries and narrowly focused programs. Our policy and management responses will need a systems approach that reflects the complexity of the natural world and the cultural values associated with it. There is little likelihood of a coherent policy emerging from the traditional compartmentalised approach in which different departments or different levels of government each handle different, small parts of a problem. It remains to be seen if the social transformations towards a sustainable future are of the order to shift governments and all sectoral interests to such a long term commitment. The future role of policy and administration at all levels of government (as well as the private sector) will be critically important to how sustainable our future might turn out to be.

Repeatedly at international gatherings, I have been struck by the common concerns of governments and communities around the world grappling with the challenges of planning for a sustainable future. Until recently these problems were broken up into small parts under the jurisdiction of individual agencies or single studies. The failure of individual sectors to solve large environmental problems has led, in recent years, to an increasing interest in collaborative, multi-disciplinary approaches to planning and management. Such collaborative approaches require a range of skills in social, economic, and scientific analysis, skills that are rarely found in one agency or one discipline. Policy makers, land managers, and natural resource scientists are being asked to create solutions to social and environmental dilemmas well beyond their expertise and experience. This book offers a partnership approach to bioregional planning applicable across the cultural mainstream of many nations.

Although specific approaches are as various as the communities in which they develop, general strategies for bioregional planning are beginning to emerge. Assessments of some evolving bioregional projects in the USA will provide valuable insights and principals for establishing future bioregional models (Gunderson et al. 1995, Johnson et al. 1999). Nations, such as the United States, Canada, Australia, and parts of Europe are beginning to develop ecoregional classifications for resource management, at least at continental scales. Later, I argue that we need to further plan to nest operational levels (cultural-bioregions) within these. Some nations of the Asia-Pacific such as New Guinea are also beginning to consider such approaches.

The occasion of a new millennium gives us the opportunity to consider new approaches to environmental problems. The scale of time represented by a millennium encourages us to find enduring solutions that transcend current political boundaries and time frames. The choices we make now form the foundation for our future beyond the next thousand years. This is not to suggest that our policies will, or even should survive forty generations. Human society, and its institutions will change as surely as the earth on which we live. Bioregional planning and management toward a sustainable future builds a resilient relationship between nature and society to face those changes. Sustaining the biosphere ultimately means that the biosphere will sustain us.

This book attempts to analyse these issues and provide at least the beginnings of a useful pathway to guide development and implementation of successful bioregional planning and management. This book, therefore, is not simply about biodiversity conservation, but about a "big picture" approach to planning and managing natural resources and ourselves in a scientifically, socially and humanly sensible way for an ecologically supportable future way beyond the next millennium.

PART I:
SCALES OF INTEGRATION: BIOSPHERE TO BIOREGIONS

CHAPTER 2

THE GLOBAL BIOSPHERE AND CONTINENTAL ECOREGIONS

Different living is not living in different places, but creating in the mind a map.

Stephen Spender, 1981

The identities and lives of the seemingly infinite varieties of plants, animals, fungi and other organisms that make up the earth's biological diversity are intrinsically intertwined. Those interactions in turn give rise to other fundamental properties that provide substantial ecological services, such as detoxification, nutrient assimilation, clean air and water (Daily 1997). While occurring across a variety of scales, these functional attributes, of which human activity is a part, collectively make up what ecologists call our biosphere. The biosphere is the veneer of life, and its support on earth and in the atmosphere.

In this chapter, I will briefly consider the issue of multiple scales or spatial contexts as they apply to multi-purpose, natural resource (and human) management. In the following chapters, I will discuss the most potent and competent implementation scale that generally reflects the requirements of ecological functions, social functions and opportunities to re-configure institutional systems for resource governance. This is the scale of biocultural landscape regions (Brunckhorst and Bridgewater 1994, Walton and Bridgewater 1996), which I refer to as bioregions.

THE BIOSPHERE AND INTERNATIONAL CONTEXT

Sustaining ecological processes, landscape function and biological diversity is an issue of importance globally, nationally and locally. Pressure to accommodate a rapidly increasing human population together with increased provision of goods and services has been growing for decades. Consequently the need for a multiple scale, trans-disciplinary approach and strategic framework for planning and managing resource use is also becoming paramount (Brunckhorst 1995, Gunderson *et al*, 1995, Berkes and Folke 1998). Pressure to take action to halt land degradation, breakdown in production systems, decreasing water quality, loss of biodiversity and global climate change has also been growing, leading national governments to commit themselves to improving the way they conserve, protect and manage ecological processes, habitats and species. While various formal international conventions are laudable, the integrated strategic planning and action necessary does not automatically follow, as the recent follow-up UNCED meeting (1997) to Rio (1993), and the Kyoto Summit (1998) on greenhouse gas emissions have plainly showed. Such instruments, though lacking international enforcement, tend to make some governments nervous and they shy away from a commitment to real action. This is particularly the case with such federated nations as Australia and the United States as well as some European and Asian countries. Successive governments in Australia have interpreted the responsibilities and our constitution (which is not unlike the USA Constitution) in different ways. For example, to protect rainforest World Heritage areas and to approve Uranium and Gold mining within excised areas of Kakadu National Park, another World heritage site. It would seem that a non-enforceable convention, though good to be seen signing, is still considered in some way threatening to national sovereignty — several recent US Senate Inquiries 1996–1999 have focused on this concern, through irrational assertions that the 'UN is taking over'. On the other hand, some governments simply know how to 'get around' or ignore any flow-on requirements from global protocols and conventions if it suits them to do so. Unfortunately, rational decision making on many of these issues appears to be dominated by economic rationalism for on-going growth and prosperity.

Global partnerships not necessarily tied to a convention, but with cross-scale, local-to-regional application, may provide valuable future directions. One such program with enormous potential is the 'Man and the Biosphere' (MAB Biosphere Reserve program) of UNESCO which is one form of bioregional planning and management seeking to integrate conservation, restoration and sustainable resource use (UNESCO 1995, Walton and Bridgewater 1996, Brunckhorst *et al.* 1997). The biosphere reserves approach is discussed further through examination of several case studies in Chapter 6.

We are told to 'Think Globally, Act Locally' (e.g., *Local Agenda 21*). While this can help focus community action, it is not really so simple. Understanding the complex functioning of the global biosphere is difficult for most people. It is especially difficult for those without enough food or freedom to contemplate a high priority to such issues. Acting locally certainly appears to effect social behavioural change, and is valuable and cost effective — especially for reusing, recycling, tree planting or other restoration activities and site specific activity by community groups. However, local action generally cannot deal with broader scale issues, arguably of greater importance, especially to eco-agricultural landscapes. In this case band-aids are applied to symptoms, for example, where rural community groups focus on very small scale projects to repair an erosion gully, or similar, without consideration of causal effects (Brunckhorst in HoRSCERA 1992, Curtis and De Lacy 1994, Reeve 1997). Issues such as global climate change, ozone depletion and *el nino* are also mysterious and remote phenomena to the general public. Neither extremes of scale really deal with the critical functional problems which are eroding productive capacities of land and sea, diminishing air and water quality and, not only adversely affecting species survival, but reducing the resilience of whole ecosystems and landscapes (Young 1995).

Sustainability and Resilience

Sustainability is a process that has ecological, social and economic dimensions. The term implies not challenging ecological thresholds on temporal and spatial scales that will negatively affect the resilience or adaptive capacities of social and ecological systems (Brunckhorst 1998). Resilience refers to the buffering capacity of a system to absorb perturbations and return to its original state. The resilient capacity of a system is the magnitude of disturbance (and its periodicity) that can be absorbed before a system changes its structure by changing processes and functional behaviour (Walker 1995, Holling *et al.* 1995, Holling 1986). Resilience within and across systems operates at multiple temporal and spatial scales. Loss of resilience undermines an ecosystem's capacity to continue to deliver life-support and other ecological services to humanity under a wide range of environmental conditions. An example of loss of resilience is illustrated through the clearing of Amazonian forests for agriculture, and, once abandoned, tend to develop into grassland or savanna and may never revert to the original forest. Similar phenomena also occur in fisheries and agriculture (Folke *et al.* 1996). Lack of resilience contributes to the failure to provide the environmental services associated with the assimilation of undesirable externalities that provides ecological buffering of human activity and resource use (Daily 1997). Richard Hobbs and colleagues, working in the highly fragmented landscapes of the Western Australian 'wheatbelt' have clearly demonstrated major alterations to ecosystem function across landscapes at a regional scale; for example, changes in the regions climate, hydrologic regimes, solar radiation balance, wind and soil movement, and species patterns (Hobbs 1993). The failure of natural resource management systems observed in recent years has been greater in magnitude than those observed historically. This change wrought by humans at a local level over time now affects very large areas easily discernible from space at a continental to global scales.

Contemporary resource management, in developed and some developing countries, has clearly failed to safeguard the dynamic capacity of ecosystems or in managing ecological and social systems for resilience and sustainability. There is considerable evidence of poor management of ecosystems with many conventional prescriptions of resource management now known to be unsustainable. Some authors attribute this fact to 'shortsightedness and greed' and question whether resources could ever be managed in a sustainable manner (Ludwick *et al.* 1993). Others argue that resource management science may be fundamentally flawed as a system of thought and practice in that its premises are based on the *laissez-faire* ideology which still persists in neo-classical economics (Daly and Cobb, 1989). Others add that it is our institutions that have failed to provide appropriate frameworks and management processes (Gunderson *et al.* 1995, Brunckhorst 1995, 1998, Hempel 1996, Power 1996, Johnson *et al.* 1999).

Resilience, like sustainability, has multi-faceted elements effecting it through scales of space and time — it does not simply occur at a local or national scale. To sustain or restore resilience in ecological and social systems for long term sustainability, we must begin to integrate our planning and operate our management across multiple scales, nesting functional requirements of ecological systems and social systems for an enduring future.

Environmental Regionalisation

Increasingly, scientists and managers are recognising the need to plan *regionally* in order to act locally. To be effective, management and local action must occur in a regionally integrated manner. While we need to use every tool and capacity we can muster to deal with such issues, they must be applied through broader strategic plans focussed on real causes not symptoms. Local community groups and individual action are essential, as are communication and partnership with them, but all our actions must be planned for scales and priorities that will contribute to maintaining ecological processes and function at larger scales. In fact we must be able to innovatively plan and manage nature and society at multiple scales — reflecting, in essence, reality. To do so and to be able to make sense of it, a hierarchy of ecological units will be required from the global biosphere to local human settlements and natural communities — 'top down' and 'bottom up'.

In order to understand its various spatial patterns, functions and scales, we can divide the biosphere into continents and oceans. Then further subdivide it into broad continental regions, regions into landscapes, landscapes into ecosystem components, and these further subdivided into patches or structural units and so on (Forman 1995, see Figures 2.3, 2.5).

While this suggestion is not entirely new, it is often difficult to keep in mind multiple spatial and temporal scales of ecological, including human, interactions. It is interesting to note that of the three levels of biodiversity described in the international convention and the *Global Biodiversity Strategy* (Courrier 1992) — genetic, species, and ecosystem — only the latter includes both biotic and abiotic interactions in space and time. The ecosystem concept is fraught with difficulty in its use because, though it is a spatial interaction of biotic and abiotic factors, it is scale-less. Ecosystem can refer to anything from microbial activity at a microscopic level within a rotting log, to that part of the log breaking down, to the whole log, to the forest or field where the log lies, to the landscape, and so on.

Building Blocks and Scale Linking Processes

Natures forms and processes are scale linking (McHaug 1969, Lyle 1985, Forman 1995). A very highly magnified view of natural forms, whether they are coastlines or organisms, will reflect minuscule, self-similar, elementary building blocks. These basic elements of form are called fractals by those who study geometric shapes in nature (see Barnsley 1988, Hastings and Sugihara 1993). Fractal geometry is based on the remarkable and unique relationship between form and its elementary building blocks. It seems to reflect and fit nature amazingly well (Barnsley 1988, Hastings and Sugihara 1993). For example, the elements of a fern frond are smaller and smaller groups of similar 'frond' shaped forms (Figure 2.1).

The connectivity of nature through multiple scales of space and time are demonstrated by fractals (Barnsley 1988, Hastings and Sugihara 1993, Van Der Ryn and Cowan 1996). Consider the hydrological cycle. A single raindrop hits the earth at the scale of millimetres. Some will be absorbed into the soil, but many more similar raindrops create a puddle that is a metre or two across. Rivulets gather (10s of metres) and flow into small streams (kilometres), which in turn feed larger and larger rivers (100s kilometres), eventually to feed oceans (1000s kilometres) and evaporate to travel the global atmosphere as water vapour.

Figure 2.1. A fern appears to be made up of smaller and smaller similar elements. These are known as fractals in geometry and represent cross scale linkages of the forms and functions of organisms and ecological systems. *(photo: D.J. Brunckhorst)*

Biosphere processes link organisms and ecological processes across jumps in scale of enormous proportions. For example the scale of photosynthesis is about one-thousandth of a millimetre; a leaf is at least ten thousand fold larger; a tree will be some thousand fold larger again; and, a forest similarly larger in proportion at a scale of hundreds of square kilometres. At each of these scales and within them, other processes and functions are occurring. Reconsider the example of the raindrop. If the droplets of water are contaminated as it falls through the atmosphere, acid rain forms. The location and excessive use of coal power generation clearly demonstrates the environmental and social costs of human activities across multiple scales. We must learn to design human activities to work with nature's scale linking systems (McHaug 1969, Lyle 1985, Van Der Ryn and Cowan 1996). To do so requires a capacity to scale up, down and across in space and time (Figure 2.2). While resource and ecosystem management will always benefit from more detailed understanding of basic elements, we must not focus so narrowly as to fragment the world — we would then not see the forested catchment for the leaves on a tree (Figure 2.2). Scaling up to a broader view helps us understand linked processes across jurisdictions and to integrate accordingly, while being careful not to lose sight of the trees for the forest (Figure 2.2).

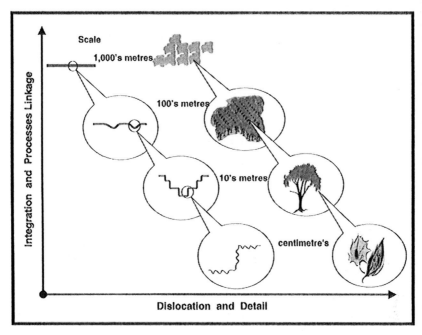

Figure 2.2. Fractals illustrate the scale linking forms and functions of nature's processes. Finer scale provides greater detail of individual elements or building blocks, but reduces our view of the connectivity of ecological systems and our ability to integrate. A broader scale reduces detail, but provides context and better integration.

Variegated Landscape Patterns and Environmental Regionalisation

At landscape to regional scales the pattern of ecological patches — a mosaic of local vegetation types, land uses and exposed geology — can be seen quite clearly from a low altitude aircraft flight. An enormous variety of ecological communities make up the veneer of life of earth. Many of these (including perhaps some of the most important) we never get to see, such as soil microbial communities, aerial, marine and freshwater plankton, and much of the oceans benthos. Patterns, however, are generally observable at many spatial scales where similar organisms or biophysical attributes occur together (Figure 2.3). We observe this pattern when internal heterogeneity is low, or homogeneity is relatively high.

Regionalisation as a process is a form of spatial classification, through which 'boundaries' are drawn around relatively homogeneous areas at a defined level of detail (spatial scale). Regionalisations are developed and applied to a range of disciplines — ecological, social, cultural and economic — to classify information, observe trends, and report and summarise patterns. Often, the kinds of attributes used reflect the question being examined in the particular discipline or specific resource being managed. The regionalisation subsequently generated may, therefore, only be useful within that discipline or management framework. Regionalisations based on numerous attributes spanning a variety of disciplines are potentially more useful as we shall observe later in this chapter.

When similar recurring ecological communities are replaced by a different set of recurring natural units, landscape boundaries can be observed and their underlying causes inferred fairly accurately. Often these represent important, rapidly changing landscape structural elements or 'steep ecotones'. Richard Forman, the doyen of landscape and regional ecology gives the following description:

> The repetition of a few characteristic ecosystems across a landscape means there is a limit on the variety of habitats available for organisms. A landscape extends in any direction until the recurring cluster of ecosystems or site types significantly changes.

(R.T.T. Forman 1995: 21)

Nested Hierarchies of Interconnected Systems

Understanding how systems of functional elements are linked at a variety of scales is referred to as hierarchy theory (Pattee 1973, O'Neill et al. 1986,

Figure 2.3. A variety of repeated landscape elements and boundary zones can be discerned in this view south of Cascade Head Research Natural Area, Oregon, USA (photo: D.J. Brunckhorst)

Forman and Godron 1986, Urban *et al.* 1987, Forman 1995). The objective of a nested hierarchy is the development of a systematic framework for classifying and mapping areas of the Earth based on the associations of ecological units at various geographic scales. A hierarchy, however, has connotations of a top-down, 'through the ranks' approach. Here, I consider it to be more like a horizontal and vertical (up and down) integration providing a nesting of similar or jointly operating features, but not in any way cutting them off from other elements or influences. A nested hierarchy of ecological units such as ecoregions, bioregions and landscapes can be a powerful tool for planning integrated terrestrial and coastal-marine management. It provides a framework for ecologically sustainable development that should be assessed in its regional, not site or local, context. Nested spatial contexts can further provide for more meaningful environmental impact assessment and more strategic planning of restoration efforts, water quality and monitoring needs, integrated catchment management, research, biodiversity assessment and integrated conservation planning. Nested spatial hierarchies can provide much needed context to implement, manage and assess actions appropriately. For example, a patch of cyanobacterial bloom in a reservoir floats amidst patches of water with no visible cyanobacteria. If we scale up, to a bird's eye view, we will see what proportion of the water body is effected. Scaling up further might provide insights into points where nutrient rich water flows into the reservoir. At a broader, landscape to regional, scale we might be able to discern patterns of land use and vegetation in the catchment, structural and functional elements, which influence water quality in the reservoir. It is often at this regional landscape level that assessment of the integration of social and ecological elements can be achieved. So a nested hierarchy of environments is useful for human planning. This is not to say however that systems operate this way — they operate within, across from bottom up, down horizontally, cycle within and across scales, and so on. Nevertheless, such a framework can be extremely useful in assessment and management of human activity and natural resources, all of which operate across and within several levels — allowing us to scale up and down, while managing across horizontally for integration and coordination. Their application and potential use is discussed in the latter chapters as we adapt and integrate social systems, institutions and governance into a new approach to environmental planning for ecologically sustainable development.

Hierarchical environmental regionalisations can help delimit areas of different biological and physical potentials and assist alternative futures analysis under various human use and resource development scenarios (e.g., Steinitz 1993, Steinitz *et al.* 1996). If we consider an area in terms of its structural and functional components, a hierarchy of landscape components can be defined (Figure 2.4). Because the units are based on a hierarchical model of ecosystem function they provide a valuable basis for making statements about the inherent levels of biological diversity, sustainable resource potential, and productivity for each region. Such an approach is fundamental to all land uses — including forestry, mining, catchment management and water quality, nature conservation, agriculture, grazing, urban planning, provision of urban/community services, and ecological restoration (McHaug 1969, Lyle 1985, Van Der Ryn and Cowan 1996).

From a structural perspective we can define a fundamental building block called a structural unit (Figure 2.4), which is an area of uniform physical characteristics such as slope, aspect and parent material. Correspondingly, each structural unit will have a series of processes attached to it, which may operate within the unit itself, influence other units, or be influenced by other factors (e.g., externalities; Brunckhorst 1998, Rollings and Brunckhorst 1999). By combining structural units

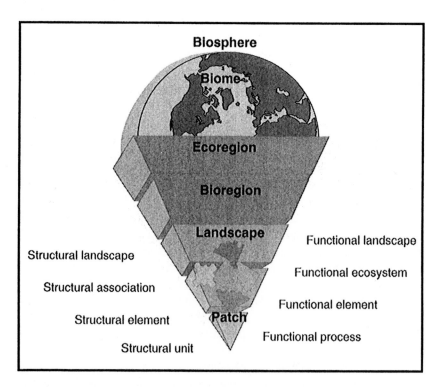

Figure 2.4. Nesting of structural and functional components of ecological units (after Rollings and Brunckhorst 1999). Human interaction with the environment occurs mainly at landscape scales, but across relatively short time periods.

together we can derive structural elements (e.g., steepness, slope, geology give terrain). Elements combine into associations, the functional equivalents of which are ecosystems. Associations can be integrated into landscapes, which correspond in scale to functional landscapes — a nested hierarchy of structure and function (Figure 2.4) across landscapes can be generated (Forman 1995). At this scale, functioning may refer to gross indicators such as productivity. In addition to spatial hierarchies, these interactions and ecological change also occur across multiple scales of time. Human interaction with the environment occurs mainly at landscape scales, but across relatively short time periods. The regional scale is the critical level at which to reconcile ecological functioning with social institutions if we are to develop novel solutions to natural resource and human sustainability (Norton and Ulanowicz 1992, 1998, Forman 1995, Kim and Weaver 1995). The model illustrated in Figure 2.4 (after Rollings and Brunckhorst, 1999) is consistent with previous classifications that are based on spatial hierarchies (e.g., Miller 1978, Forman and Godron 1986, Forman 1995, Omernik 1995,1997, Bailey 1996).

We should keep in mind, however, that humans derive ecological classifications and mapping systems in an attempt to meet human needs — often questions focused on a single issue or resource. Ecological systems and their various components inclusive of natural resources form continua, often changing only gradually, but edges can be sharp such as the boundary between patches of forest and pasture. Whether sharply defined or much more gradual, these ecotones can be critical areas for management or maintenance of broader ecological processes (such as dispersal of meta-populations of species) and for governing human activity.

Natural resource management for an ecologically supportable future requires examination of multiple spatial scales of ecological interactions and human activity. When planning to manage human interactions with land and sea resources in a sustainable way, a nested hierarchy of ecosystem units is required (Slocombe 1993, Omernik 1995, Bailey 1996, Papadimitriou and Mairota 1996, Holling and Meffe 1996).

FROM GLOBAL TO CONTINENTAL TO ECOLOGICAL REGIONS

It is necessary to build a framework that can bridge the critical gap from local to global, but which is still practical to implement at local, national and continental levels of social and ecological organisation (Brunckhorst 1998b). The vision for such a framework and its ultimate creation will require an enormous amount of cooperation at all these levels to facilitate not only ownership, but responsibility for each part of a jigsaw, each having pieces within pieces (Figure 2.5). This development of such a global-to-local framework would provide a scientifically sound, and socio-economically pragmatic regionalisation of the biosphere at a variety of nested scales of ecological function for natural resource planning and management across jurisdictional boundaries. It can start being developed at several levels from the top-down, the middle-out, and from the bottom-up.

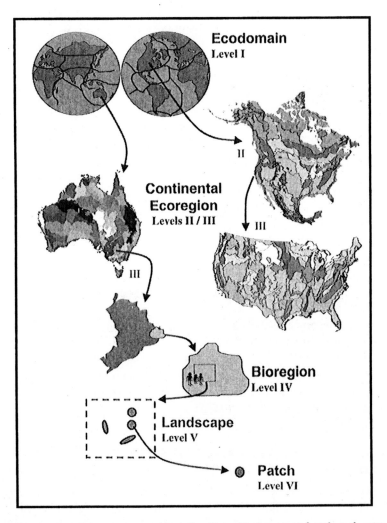

Figure 2.5. Diagrammatic representation of a hierarchical system of ecological units for natural resource management (Ecoregional classifications of Australia, North America and USA from Thackway and Cresswell eds. 1995 and, courtesy J. Omernik US EPA, US Geological Survey EROS Data Centre, Environment Canada, Mexico Institute for Ecology and Commission for Environmental Cooperation 1997).

Nesting of Environmental Regions

Initial research and development activity has produced several classifications and maps at the continental ecoregional level (e.g., Bailey *et al.* 1985, Wiken 1986, Omernik 1987, 1997, Bailey 1989, Thackway and Cresswell 1995, Marshall *et al.* 1996). These regionalisations, which attempt to focus on multiple biodiversity and resource management purposes, differ notably from specific purpose or single use environmental classifications such as forestry alone, water quality or expanding conservation reserve alone (e.g., Bailey 1976, Thackway and Cresswell eds, 1993, 1995). Different single purpose environmental classifications used by different agencies duplicate effort and exacerbate our inability to coordinate natural resource management efforts. In essence, the latter paradigm defeats the ultimate aim of dealing with the whole variety of nature, society and human activity including various forms of resource use and conservation strategies (see Omernik and Gallant 1990, Omernik 1995, Omernik and Bailey 1997 for discussion).

It is necessary to reconcile all these purposes across landscapes and ecosystems in order to work towards integrated and sustainable conservation and production. Clearly, single purpose and single scale environmental classifications do not do this and will tend not to be widely used for integrated, multiple resource management. Hence, it is worth emphasising that developing environmental contexts such as bioregional frameworks will only be of value if they are meaningful for planning and management across political jurisdictions and can integrate multiple resource sectors or land uses. This requires cross-jurisdictional, cross-sectoral and inter-agency ownership, and identity with and responsibility for the bioregion. Furthermore, the delimited bioregional context should match or approximate in some way the identity and understanding that local communities have of the landscape environment in which they live and work (Kaus 1993, Kim and Weaver 1994, Brunckhorst 1995, 1998). While this might be a problem in areas where there is a very high rate of turnover of itinerants (e.g., refugees or immigrants who don't settle), in most areas the local community is a temporal mix of very long term (inter-generational) and medium term residents, together with short to medium term itinerants.

For ecological regionalisations to be generally applicable to a wide range of resource and environmental planning activities (e.g., from local government to international agreements), they require synthesis of a wide range of biological, physical and social attributes which reflect the character of ecological systems and processes at landscape scales. Similar approaches have developed in parallel in several countries (Canada, Wiken 1986; USA, Bailey 1976, Omernik 1987, 1997, Omernik and Gallant 1990; Australia,

Thackway and Cresswell eds. 1995; Great Britain, Bunce et al. 1996).

Omernik (1995) emphasises the value of this new integrated approach to the identification of ecoregions/bioregions in the following way:

> ... the difference between this approach to defining ecoregions and most preceding methods is based on the hypothesis that ecological regions gain their identity through spatial differences in a combination of landscape characteristics. One of the strengths of the approach lies in the analysis of multiple geographic characteristics that are believed to cause or reflect differences in the mosaic of ecosystems, including their potential composition.
>
> Omernik (1995: 52)

In Australia, the Interim Biogeographic Regionalisation of Australia (compiled by Thackway and Cresswell eds. 1995), a continental scale ecoregional classification (Level III) was, at first, mistakenly considered a single scale, single use regionalisation intended only for conservation reserve assessment because it was initially developed for that single purpose. However, it actually incorporated multiple data sets of ecosystem and landscape characteristics and a combination of quantitative and qualitative synthesis, across scales. Through its development in partnership with a variety of State and local resource management agencies it gained broad acceptance through several levels of government and some community groups. Subsequently, it has become of wider interest to many public and private resource and land management agencies. It has also provided a basis for assessment of more pragmatic bioregional (level IV) frameworks for local communities to integrate restoration, catchment management and sustainable land use planning together with local authorities.

Environment Canada has been a leader in developing holistic, multi-purpose regionalisations (e.g., Wiken 1986, Marshall et al. 1996). Wiken (1986) outlines the Canadian approach, noting that the ecologically distinct areas can be seen as a mostly systems resulting from the interaction of geologic, soil, landform, vegetative, climatic, flora and fauna, water and human factors which may be present. The dominance of any factor will vary within each ecological area. He also points out that such an inclusive and integrative approach to describing ecosystem regionality, including human influences, can be applied iteratively across scales from very broad landscape systems to site specific ecosystems (Wiken 1986).

It would appear that real advances towards the vision for a 'global-to-local' framework illustrated in Figure 2.5, are on a threshold. More work, however, is needed to translate these approaches into a flexible, but explicit, system of nomenclature and scales for various levels of regionalisation.

Rather than 'reinvent' some of these, I would like to use some existing terms for classifications to synthesise an acceptable framework and strategy across nations and globally. The following ecological hierarchy framework (Table 2.1) adapts Omernik's practical ecoregion framework (Omernik 1987, 1995, 1997, Omernik *et al.* 1997, Bryce and Clarke 1996), and expands it to six levels. For wider application and development, I need to clarify the natural resource management area, ranges of appropriate scale for mapping, and a system of nomenclature for the regions at various levels. Table 2.1 summarises these features and their attributes.

TABLE 2.1.

Hierarchical framework of ecological units for natural resource management from global to local scales (Levels and nomenclature correspond to Figure 2.5).

Hierarchy Level	Name	Planning and Management Area	Mapping Scale (range)	
I	Ecodomain	global biosphere, inter-continental	> 1: 20, 000, 000	⬆
II / III	Ecoregion	continental / sub-continental	1: 20, 000, 000 to 1: 5, 000, 000	Ecosystem Function
IV	Bioregion	regional landscapes	1: 5, 000, 000 to 1: 250, 000	
V	Landscape	sub-regional, landscape ecosystems	1: 250, 000 to 1: 25, 000	
VI	Patch	ecosystem component	1: 25,000 to 1: 5, 000	⬇

The first level of regionalisation of the biosphere is termed an Ecodomain (Table 2.1, Figure 2.5). This extremely broad region could encompass large parts of one or more continents or sub-continents and probably portions of ocean realms. Climatic attributes are the primary driving forces at the broad Ecodomain level, but major geological patterns also contribute to these ecological units; for example, Arctic Polar, Antarctic Polar, Sub-Antarctic, Humid Tropics, Sub-Tropics.

Geomorphology and climate are major influences to ecoregional scales of regionalisation (Levels II, Continental and III, Sub-Continental; Table 2.1). Two levels are necessary because of the scales of magnitude and variability of continental landmasses and the oceans. For example, the USA and Australia are about the same size, but the scale and magnitude of their continental context is quite different. A level II regionalisation of North America is useful for bridging the global scale ecodomains of this vast continent. A level III regionalisation becomes a further breakdown in the hierarchy (or it might be useful to meld the two levels). In Australia, level II is unnecessary and the *Interim Biogeographic Regionalisation of Australia* (Thackway and Cresswell 1995) portrays level III continental ecoregions (see Figure 2.5).

Bioregions nest within this system at about level IV. They are spatially congruent sets of similar landscape ecosystems with which local people (rural, urban, indigenous communities) identify. They provide sensible planning and management contexts, essentially reflecting nature (ecological functioning) and society (social and institutional functioning) (Courrier ed., 1992, Brunckhorst 1994, 1995, 1998, Miller 1996, Batisse 1996, Brunckhorst and Rollings 1998). The application of bioregional planning and management within and across bioregions are discussed in the following chapters.

While several countries have recently undertaken or are now undertaking ecoregional classifications at the continental/sub-continental scale (level III), very few have been developed that nest landscapes (level V) within bioregions (level IV) within ecoregions (II/III). The regional context offered by bioregions (IV) and landscapes (V), however, are now being recognised as the critical scales for managing whole interconnected systems along with managing human activity, land use and resource governance (Bromley 1992, Norton and Ulanowicz 1992, Hansen and di Castri 1992, HoRSCERA 1992, 1993, Brunckhorst and Bridgwater 1994, Dutton and Saenger, 1994, Kim and Weaver 1994, Brunckhorst 1998a, b, Walton and Bridgewater 1996).

The landscape level V unit for management (Table 2.1) reduces the variability within bioregions further down to local social and biophysical characteristics (including land use attributes; urban landscapes) and repeated small patches of ecological units (biopatches) across the landscape. A landscape is often a mix of similar local ecosystems and land uses reflecting clearly the three spatial elements — patch, corridor and matrix (Forman and Godron 1981, Forman 1995). This level in the hierarchy has also been found to be useful in reconciling a better environmental context for local stream and sub-catchment management in concert with managing land use at a local scale (e.g., Bryce and Clarke 1996).

The level VI, patch, contains the finest detail in the hierarchical framework of ecological units (Figure 2.5, Table 2.1). These are the elements within a fragmented or variegated landscape, but not excluding linear patches such as riparian areas along streams (Forman 1995). Patches might be a woodlot, patch of remnant vegetation, a field of wheat or, a localised infestation of weeds (e.g., blackberry in Australia, *Melaleuca/ Eucalyptus* in the United States).

Integration and Focus: Scaling Up and Scaling Down

By organising the complexity of the biosphere at appropriate scales and nested ecological frameworks, a local to global planning and management approach can become a powerful tool to integrate and coordinate a wealth of capacities and activities towards an ecologically supportable future. The global scale is important internationally if we are to deal with sustaining the biosphere and allow atmospheric balances to recover. Clearly, however, it is too broad with too little detail to implement ecosystem management at appropriate land use and social scales to match ecosystems and ecological function of landscapes. At a local level there is sometimes too much detail which we then fragment in order to deal with it — connectivity becomes obscured and actions become band-aids on symptoms rather than integrated solutions to causes — and fragmented decision making promotes crisis management (Gunderson *et al.* 1995).

The ability, however, to scale-up and scale-down for assessment and temporal adjustment supports the idea of a nested hierarchy of management units from local to global. In North America, the international Great Lakes ecoregion is an example of several nested management zones and cooperative mechanisms moving from a huge basin-wide regional strategy down through individual lake management plans to local area remedial action plans. This nested hierarchy for strategic planning may be a key element in the relative success of the evolving bioregional Great Lakes management. In contrast, the Columbia River Basin is a vast ecoregional-scale ecosystem management project, which seems almost too big to handle. The ecoregion has been effectively subdivided into well over 100 sub-basins for scaling environmental information, but these do not necessarily reflect local communities' identity with regional landscapes within the basin. The struggles to date to implement management changes in the basin might reflect the inability of planning frameworks to reconcile social and scientific understanding of the landscape (Johnson *et al.* 1998)._

While working through multiple scales is clearly important, we need to identify strategic operational scales to plan for management of enduring adaptive ecological and social systems that recognise that political economy is a subset of the environment. The bioregional scale of integration across regional landscapes incorporates ecological, social, governance and corporate elements (Slocombe 1993, Chapter 3). Bioregions, therefore become the operationally efficient framework in planning for integrated management. Temporal scales are important in collective action to deal with all kinds of change (ecological, social, economic, organisational), along with the collective knowledge of place, development of long-term commitment and its subsequent transfer to new institutions and future generations. This suggests a subtle process of adaptive management of which we are generally unaware, but which requires and sustains the necessary social and institutional flexibility for future change and adaptation (Chapters 4 and 5).

CHAPTER 3

BIOREGIONS AS BIOCULTURAL LANDSCAPES

Although ecology may be treated as science, its greater and overriding wisdom is universal ... That wisdom can be approached mathematically, chemically, or it can be danced or told as a myth ... a deep sense of engagement with the landscape, with profound connections to surroundings and to natural processes central to life.

Paul Shepard, 1969

A bioregion is an integration of human governance with ecological law. It is an operationally pragmatic context that matches the functions and requirements of culture and society with ecological processes, services and functions. A bioregional framework for planning and managing ourselves helps us understand and develop an enduring relationship within ecological law — the rules and conditions necessary to sustain biodiversity and ecosystem processes. As Paul Shepard suggests, wisdom is required to harmonise the relationship of a currently rapacious society within the ecological potential of the landscapes where we live.

Landscapes and seascapes are not just visual symbols of natural or human environments; rather, they are agents of cultural power by which social and subjective identities evolve (Brunckhorst 1995, Weeks 1996). Human inhabitants have generally modified their landscapes to meet a desired need and, as a result, identify very strongly (though perhaps unconsciously) with that landscape. Examples include, the use of fire by American and Australian indigenous peoples, subsistence agricultures of

Asia and South America, and Eurocentric styles of agriculture and grazing. In Australia and the USA, intensive development for wheat farming or cotton growing has removed native grazers and high-order predators from rain-fed native grasslands and deserts, which are now irrigated. In today's world, most landscapes are obviously anthropocentric having long been subjected to human influences. As a result of these increasingly institutionalised and extensive land-use changes, it is clear that natural landscape boundaries and ecotones are not in harmony with political boundaries or the economies of production (Power 1996). In contrast, but perhaps not surprising, is the increasing use of such terms as 'biocultural landscape' or 'bioregion' to explain the real, but cognitively lost, linkage between humans and landscape ecosystems. A pragmatic and operationally useful landscape-scale context is required to draw these natural-social elements together to assist the institutional learning and paradigmatic shift towards planning and management for a sustainable future. It might be argued that a bioregional framework should reflect geographical distribution of ecological attributes and processes. Lines on maps around strict biological or physical earth properties (i.e., strict environmental classification), however, are unlikely to be heeded by most people or institutions, let alone the natural resource users, policy makers and managers of land and sea. Indeed, this has been the lesson learnt in the past decade in Australia, Canada and the USA (Chapter 2).

Mumford (1938) writing some 60 years ago articulated the notion, that to be useful, a region had to be a balanced concept. One which is not simply a purely scientific and environmentally deterministic view, nor one which gives no regard to the land or its ecology. Noting that any spatial definition of 'region' is a human construct irrespective of rigorous quantitative methodology, he suggested that a dialectical view of regions as the most useful, and probably the most accurate.

> The human region ... is a complex of geographic, economic, and cultural elements. Not found as a finished product in nature, not solely the creation of human will and fantasy, the region, like its corresponding artefact, the city, is a collective work of art.

Lewis Mumford 1938: 367

People living in local communities (e.g., a small valley) will tend to have much weaker identification with very large regions such as, the Great Lakes of North America or the extensive Murray-Darling Basin of Australia (both regions might better be considered at the continental ecoregional scale described in Chapter 2). If local people do not identify to a reasonably high degree with their bioregion, it is unlikely to serve as a strategic planning and management framework for sustainability goals. Therefore, I consider 'bioregion' to be synonymous with 'cultural bioregion' (a region of similar biocultural landscapes; Box 3.1). Essentially a bioregion is made up of adjacent similar landscape ecosystems with which local human communities identify because of how they see it, use it, and what it produces for them — whether mostly natural or modified to varying degrees (Courrier 1992, Brunckhorst and Bridgewater 1995, Weeks 1996, Schoonmaker et al. 1996). Recognition that humans and their communities and resource use are a part of, shape and build identities with their regional landscape is inherent in my definition of a bioregion (a level IV region; see Chapter 2, Figure 2.3). Therefore the concept promoted here differs from a strict environmental classification and with the small, closed, self-sufficient community espoused by bioregionalists (see Sale 1985, Chernyi 1986, Alexander 1990). Landscape design theory has perhaps best been espoused by visionary authors such as McHaug (1969), Lyle (1985), Forman (1995) and Stieniz (1993). A biocultural context for design of regional landscapes for planning and managing an enduring future for both nature and society leads to a bioregional framework described herein. I see a bioregion as crossing or encompassing political jurisdictional boundaries and necessary to best plan and manage on a holistic local-regional basis that matches landscape scale ecological function with social/cultural features and functioning within and across such regions (Brunckhorst 1995, 1998). In this sense, Jensen's (1994) description of bioregional councils in California fits with my concept of a functional bioregion. The valuable case studies of 'bioregions' reviewed in Schoonmaker et al. (1997) and Johnson et al. (1999) are generally broader (e.g., the Pacific North-West or Great Lakes regions), matching the ecoregional level (level III), but give some attention to bioregional scales (level IV, Chapter 2) in the sense that I consider them here.

Social Function and Bioregions

The structure and function of ecological systems has a vast range of complex scale issues. In Chapter 2, I briefly examined the concept of nested hierarchies of biophysical systems. Social systems are not only complex, but also convoluted in terms of scale issues across space and time (Hagget et al. 1977). Hierarchies are still a feature of society today even though we have moved much more towards distributed networks of social organisation. Many societal elements such as families, corporations and government agencies predominantly operate in a top down hierarchical manner. One basic building block in society is still generally considered to be the family (comprising individuals), social norms are then built around the home environment and then a widening circle of interactions with friends/neighbours, education/communication, citizenry/government and work/land use. These might be influenced by a variety of factors such as a set of spiritual beliefs, the neighbourhood, peers, behavioural norms, and a sense of community built. However, contemporary society is influenced and built by a much greater range of factors often operating horizontally (Meidinger 1997, 1998). Globalisation in all forms, including trade and powerful multi-national companies contribute to the shape of social systems. Multiple layers of government, administrative arrangements and infrastructure (e.g., roads, urban services) are probably the main cause of convolutions and overlapping (or competing) institutional requirements (Caldwell 1970, Bromerly 1991, Ostrom 1990, Brunckhorst 1998). These top-down political structures again give rise to problems of policy coordination across levels, fragmented sectoral based resource management. Institutional impediments are described further in Chapter 4 and the benefits of a bioregional approach for participatory development of cross-sectoral coordination and multi-level governance considered.

Society and how it functions is essentially a reflection of its dynamic nature as a continually emerging process (Shannon 1992). The process of defining the networks of social, cultural, economic and political boundaries is what creates the loose boundaries of social organisation and community. It seems that in reality a continuous variety of interactions and change — up/down, horizontally and at multiple scales — shapes society. We all play some role in creating the social configuration within which we also live. Various case studies suggest that 'policy communities' or 'communities of common concern', which are loosely organised, local-regional, social networks allow innovation for development of new institutional forms and organisational arrangements to pursue social and ecological sustainability (Gunderson *et al.* 1995, Shannon 1998, Johnson *et al.* 1999). Most of these features have a spatial context in which they sit and, indeed, often have a wider area of influence on both social and ecological processes (Meidinger 1997, Brunckhorst and Rollings 1999). These can be mapped in multiple layers on a Geographical Information System. Similarly, the zone or extent of regulatory mechanisms and administrative arrangements can also be spatially represented (Rollings and Brunckhorst 1999). The structure and function of spiritual beliefs may be difficult to represent spatially because of their cognitive and interpretive nature, but they do affect human value systems and how we identify with and interpret our surroundings, our sense of 'place', and resource management (Berkes and Folke 1998, Shannon 1998).

Social processes can take a variety of forms and occur at a variety of scales. For example their strength and direction, weakening or spreading, and rate of change or cycling through time. Data that are gathered by a population census might help to spatially frame a social context. Mapping of land use, rural social networks and personal feelings of some identity with landscape features are equally important. Carl Steinitz and colleagues have developed methods for spatial analysis for alternative planning scenarios across regional landscapes to assess futures scenarios (Steinitz 1993, Steinitz et al. 1996). Constraints, opportunities and responsibilities that pertain to land uses that envelope both social and ecological functions, as a consequence of the bodies of common law, statute law and associated scheduled regulations administered by Federal, State and Municipal agencies, will be useful in auditing and defining new governance systems (Brown and MacLeod 1996, Brunckhorst and Rollings 1999). This is necessary if duplication of existing functions of government and agencies is to be avoided, and when new resource governance models modify or replace existing institutions (e.g., Gunderson et al. 1995, Johnson et al. 1999). This understanding can provide an integrated (cultural) bioregional context to plan and manage for integrated conservation and sustainable resource use (Figure 3.1). Policies and institutions for natural resource management might then be planned and integrated for appropriate configurations (Armitage 1995, Norton and Dovers 1996, Holling and Meffe 1996, Meidinger 1997, 1998).

A bioregional framework for planning and managing resource conservation and use must reflect both, ecological functional processes and social processes. It provides the appropriate matching context for integration. This geographic 'place' integrates the multiple capacities of social systems to define values and achieve common goals compatible with ecological capacity at multiple scales (Figure 3.1). The actions and choices of local human communities interacting with the ecological systems of the local landscape affect a 'place' and give rise to its social identity (Shannon 1992, 1998). Local level community governance and collective action for sustainability requires a 'natural' nesting of society with landscape scale ecosystem processes — human communities identifying with the dynamic natural capital of the place in which they live and the nurturing responsibility and capacities to sustain it — the essence of a Bioregion (Figure 3.1).

DEFINING A STRATEGIC BIOREGIONAL FRAMEWORK

The best science cannot maintain ecosystems and functional processes unless they are incorporated into the human social domain (Saunders 1990, Reeve, 1992, Norton and Ulanowicz 1992, Heinen 1995, Weeks 1996). The connectivities of nature already exist — we need human management

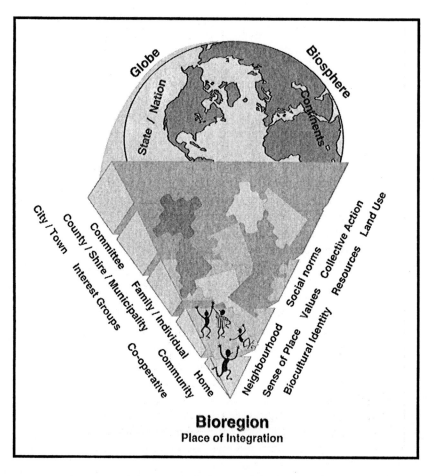

Figure 3.1. The nesting of dynamic social systems with landscape scale ecosystem processes allows for emergent relationships of organisation and governance to reflect a geographical 'place'. This is the essence of a Bioregion — giving rise to local level community governance and collective action for sustainability, including the responsibility and capacities for stewardship — the Place of Integration (in part, after Shannon 1992, 1998, Rollings and Brunckhorst 1999).

systems that reflect these natural processes — a bioregional planning framework can help achieve these common goals (Gunderson *et al.* 1995, Brunckhorst 1995, 1998, Samson and Knopf 1996). Furthermore, public resource managers in particular, will increasingly attribute little relevance to academically intriguing studies if there is no baseline information presented in a spatial context to ground their understanding. This requires integration of social and ecological elements at relevant spatial and temporal scales.

There is no landscape, nor any part of the biosphere (and atmosphere) that remains without some influence of human activity. Natural regions have begun to give way in people's lives to regions important for their social function. Yet, the nexus of 'natural' landscape regions with 'social' ones provides a strategic opportunity. We should endeavour to take advantage of the potential for using 'ecologically and culturally functional' landscape regions (bioregions) as vehicles for developing and managing for ecological sustainability and social responsibility — modifying human activity and institutions in the process. If developed and understood in this way, bioregional frameworks for planning and management have the capacity to become successful, adaptive experimental management contexts for sustainability (Box 3.1). They will also be scientifically and politically defensible. Within a bioregional framework for planning and management, uncertainty (or lack of knowledge) about the status and function of

---

Box 3.1 Definitions for the Application of Bioregional Planning Concepts

(after Courrier 1992, Brunckhorst 1994, 1995)

The term *Bioregion* refers to an area of land and/or water whose limits are defined not by political boundaries, but by the geographical distribution of biophysical attributes, ecological systems and human communities. These are 'practical' domains for planning and management purposes. Bioregions need to be a 'recognisable' similar environment/s to the people that live, work, recreate and use resources there.

Bioregional planning is a planning framework which allows for the variously defined and tenured areas of land or sea within a bioregion to be managed in a complementary way to achieve long-term conservation, resource use and human lifestyle objectives in concert with local communities.

Future productivity from land (and sea) will depend on how the entire landscape is used and managed. In order to pursue a sustainable future, human needs and activities must be integrated with broader scale ecosystem management that maintains biodiversity and ecological services – towns, farms, forests, pastoral land and fisheries belong on the same planning array as reserves, species conservation, water management and land restoration. This integrative approach to adaptive management is *Bioregional Management*.

ecological systems can be incorporated into an adaptive management strategy — an approach that relies on continual assessment and adjustment (Walters 1986, Walters and Holling 1990). These aspects are discussed in more detail in the following Chapters.

DEVELOPING AN OPERATIONAL FRAMEWORK

A major objective of bioregional planning and management is to facilitate the development of culturally appropriate local and regional systems of resource governance that match resource use and conservation to the bioregional capacity to provide resources and ecosystem services (Brunckhorst 1998). To successfully maintain nature and society, a bioregional framework must integrate not only multiple, but operational, scales of ecosystems, tenure, law and resource use such that ecologically detrimental externalities of human activity are halted and reversed. The capacity of regional ecological systems to generate primary products and satisfy social values depends on the amount of energy captured and the use and rotation of nutrients in the constituent soil base. For sustainability, human activity in harvesting the produce must be tempered to an ecologically supportable level — withdrawal of the 'interest' while maintaining the (natural) capital base and, ecological processes and services that support it (Barbier 1993, Daily 1997).

A synthesis of desirable and locally meaningful characteristics is therefore required in a bioregional planning framework to integrate environmental and sustainable development objectives (Dyer and Holland 1991, Slocombe, 1993, Brunckhorst 1995). We have seen in Chapter 2 that pure environmental classifications are unlikely to achieve this. The multi-disciplinarity of landscape ecology however, can greatly assist coupling biodiversity and ecosystem function with production systems and larger scale processes to guide coordination of policies, management and social programs towards sustainable land and sea uses (Steinitz 1993, Kim and Weaver 1994). The mosaic of landscapes in a region affects not just that region but neighbouring and perhaps more distant ones as well. Public policies may, in turn, affect various regions in similar, variable or synergistic ways, emphasising that linkages within and between bioregions are both institutional and biophysical. The bioregional framework entails multi-stakeholder groups working at a local level to establish co-operative programs that address ecological, cultural and economic issues at the scale of the regional landscape — a modern form of participatory democracy for sustainable resource governance (Heinen 1995, Western et al. eds 1996, Brunckhorst et al. 1997, Folke and Berkes 1998).

A generalised view of the spatial scale of various biophysical and societal features is given in Figure 3.2 (after Slocombe 1993). The landscape-regional scale of a bioregion combines the various scales of human interactions with biophysical elements operating at a variety of other scales (Figure 3.2). In doing so the bioregional framework envelopes and reshapes social institutions for resource governance drawing together multi- and cross- scale attributes so that human needs and activities are reconciled and integrated with ecological structural and functional processes (Brunckhorst 1995, 1998). Hence, a bioregion, 'biocultural landscape' or 'life region' integrates human governance within ecological law. It is an area exhibiting 'soft perimeters' characterised by its drainage, flora and fauna, climate, geology, human culture and land use.

Bioregions, ecoregions and other regions in the hierarchy (Chapter 2) are therefore general contextual frameworks for natural resource planning and management, and biodiversity conservation. Any kind of regionalisation is a human construct no-matter how it is built, but its value lies in its acceptance and usefulness rather than how accurately its 'boundary' line is placed between differing attributes (see Griffith *et al.* 1994, Omernik 1995, Omernik and Bailey 1997). Acceptance and use will reflect how well the

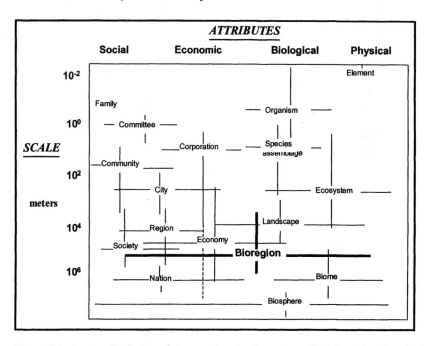

Figure 3.2. A generalised view of the spatial scale of a variety of biophysical and societal attributes indicating the bridging between socio-economic and ecological attributes offered by a strategic bioregional context. The dashed line reminds us that multi-national corporations have a global scale of operation and influence (adapted after Slocombe 1993).

geographic context matches social structuration of a sense of 'place' as a nested geographic context for integration and coordination of activity (Figure 3.1). As such, the 'biocultural' landscape level of a bioregional framework can provide a valuable basis for a regional-landscape assessment of a range of alternative land use scenarios and their possible consequences (Steinitz 1993, Steinitz et al. 1996, Johnson et al. 1999). These can then be used to guide bioregional planning for sustainable futures.

We now need to revisit the notion presented in Chapter 1 (Figure 1.1) of the dominant paradigm which sees the environment as a subset of the economy (along with society). The task is to elaborate a workable solution that can help shift this emphasis to the more sustainable position, not losing sight of societal needs, of the economy within society within the conditions for sustaining the biosphere (Figure 3.3).

To design and implement a strategic bioregional framework, a dynamic and interactive process is required. Pragmatic identification of 'loose', but useful, boundaries will be achieved through coupling of explicit biophysical regionalisation and resource capacity to reflect ecological functional processes, and reconfiguring these with the social-cultural identity of human communities living in that environment and the social functions reflecting that geographical place. This must be an iterative and flexible process involving the use of qualitative and quantitative information

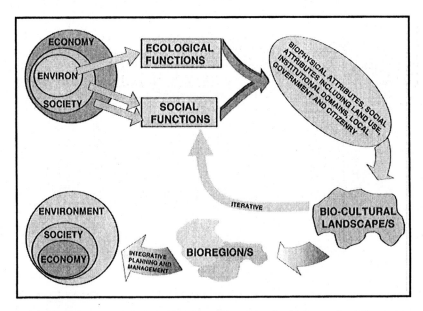

Figure 3.3. Conceptual diagram of major elements in developing and implementing a bioregional framework for strategic planning and management. Bioregional planning will in turn facilitate emergence of more adaptable and ecologically sustaining governance institutions.

assimilation, and wide consultation with resource managers, government agencies, civic governors (local, municipal, county councils), as well as other community groups and citizens (Figure 3.3).

Bioregional planning must become a key mechanism for developing ecologically sustainable and adaptable governance institutions for an enduring future. A bioregion provides an integration of human governance with ecological connectivity at multiple scales. It is a geographic 'place' exhibiting 'soft perimeters' characterised by its drainage, flora and fauna, climate, geology, human culture, social organisation and land use. Bioregions provide an operationally pragmatic context that matches the functions and requirements of society (communities) with ecological processes, services and functions. A bioregional framework facilitates integration of all levels of social organisation into effective governance processes for an enduring relationship with ecosystems at multiple levels — from small ecological communities, to landscape ecosystems to regional landscapes to the biosphere and atmosphere. The bioregional framework envelopes and reshapes social institutions for resource governance drawing together multi- and cross- scale attributes so that human needs and activities are reconciled and integrated with ecological structural and functional processes (Brunckhorst 1995, 1998). The ecoregion (Level II and III) is a broader context in which bioregions nest providing a further level of horizontal integration (Chapter 2).

In facilitating cultural and institutional shifts towards more inclusive, holistic and strategic planning and management it will be necessary to provide a pathway for change. Time is required for rebuilding and adapting to new institutional forms. This will be assisted by a form of social adaptive management, including iterative steps as indicated in the simplified schematic shown in Figure 3.3. Managing transformations at various levels of structural institutions (corporate and government) and re-assigning a collective responsibility in real partnership with citizens will be the greatest challenge to establishing operational bioregional frameworks. The next section examines some of the institutional barriers to be overcome and some potential solutions.

PART II:
SOCIAL AND
INSTITUTIONAL ADAPTION

CHAPTER 4

INSTITUTIONAL IMPEDIMENTS: BIOREGIONAL SOLUTIONS

We need to understand how much of our lives are lived in and through institutions and how better institutions are essential if we are to lead better lives. In surveying our present institutions we need to discern what is healthy in them and what needs to be altered, particularly where we have begun to destroy the non-renewable natural and nearly non-renewable human resources upon which all our institutions depend.

Bellah *et al.* 1991: 5

Value systems, behavioural norms and institutions are all interconnected. Past values and 'acceptable' social practices shaped our current institutions and changing social values will drive the evolution of future institutions. I use the term 'institution' in the broad sense to include social norms, customs and practices, as well as more formally structured institutions such as government, agencies and private or corporate organisations. Understandably, many of our current institutions developed to serve quite different purposes, rather than for collectively managing natural resources and ourselves in a sustainable manner at multiple spatial and temporal scales. The fundamental question is whether current institutions have outlived their usefulness. Are existing institutions flexible enough to adapt to large-scale (and multiple-scale) ecosystem management approaches, or are new institutions required? For example, it has become an institution throughout much of the USA, Australia, and elsewhere to emphasise the rights of the individual over the longer-term interests of the community.

This attitude is unlikely to contribute to values for long-term sustainability and intergenerational equity.

In contrast to the seeming unsustainability of some of our modern institutions, our basic understanding of ecosystems has been built through a very long period of human interactions and 'negotiations' with the surrounding environment (Bird 1987). Environments have been modified since before recorded time to provide the goods most valued by the community. To become normalised in society, such values (and such modifications) must have been perceived to be in the long-term interests of the people and their descendants. It would seem, however, that much of modern natural resource management practices, policies or ethos ignore the long-term interests of people and their descendants and run counter to biological and cultural reality. How this may have evolved is unclear. The perceived failure of commons led to new failures of privatisation and externalised costs. Regulation strangled innovation. Institutions (both as cultural norms and as structured agencies) no longer were agents of ecological and social sustainability.

The entry of the disciplines of landscape ecology and ecosystem management into the arena of natural resources policy is a step in the right direction, but has not been without difficulties (Norton and Ulanowicz 1992, Grumbine 1994, Norton and Dovers 1996, Meidinger 1997). People traditionally responsible for policy, law, planning, and infrastructure developments (politicians, bureaucrats, social scientists, lawyers and engineers) generally have little or no training in ecology. Likewise, ecologists tend to be equally ill-equipped to understand social needs, policy, finance or planning. Knowledge is not the main problem: Institutional impediments are a larger barrier to implementation of critically necessary, inter-disciplinary and cross-jurisdictional resource management at regional, continental and global scales.

INSTITUTIONAL INADEQUACY

Many practical solutions to the sustainable use of natural resources are constrained by enslaved institutions such as private property rights and government subsidy, or by institutional limitations, such as narrowly focused scientific research and entrenched or compartmentalised systems of resource governance (Kim and Weaver 1994, Holling and Meffe 1996). In essence, institutional inadequacy stems from relying on old institutional baggage to solve new classes of problems — a lack of adaptation. For example, in Australia and the USA, our inherited European styles of agriculture and land ownership do not always match the biophysical nature of our lands, and have become major barriers to the pursuit of sustainability at the necessary, cross-jurisdictional, landscape scale. Yet this remains a very hard institution to change. Rural areas, in particular, are dual entities, private production systems and a tradeable commodity on one hand, but also part of an interconnected ecosystem across a landscape with no regard to ownership limits (Reeve 1992, 1997, Samson and Knopf 1996, Meidinger 1998). To address broader scale, long-term sustainability, narrowly confined land use approaches that manage for one particular production purpose perform poorly in considering ecological and social connectivity across components of the landscape systems in which they occur (Holling and Meffe 1996, Brown and MacLeod 1996, Brunckhorst 1998).

Political Economy

Many of the impediments to holistic ecosystem management are driven by economic institutions, especially 'the free market'. It is unlikely that ecosystems can ever be appropriately priced by markets. Ecological services and processes such as nutrient cycling, assimilation of toxins, cleansing water and air, climate and hydrological cycles, pollination of plants are grossly unpriced by markets. Meidinger (1997, 1998) noted that there are no buyers willing to pay the full value of these ecological functions and that many beneficiaries of these ecosystem services, such as future human and non-human generations, cannot partake in the current market. Ecological processes and ecosystem services of benefit to such groups will continue to be undervalued by markets (Meidinger 1997).

Economically rational policies tend to command governments. Environmental costs of rural production or delivery of urban services are rarely accounted for despite the growing interest in ecological economics and environmental accounting (Barbier 1993). Governments subsidise extensive infrastructure development for resource access and use; but it is inevitable that the economic and ecological costs are too high, and eventually lead to social as well as environmental degradation (Power 1996). The required model for decision making must view economics as a subset of society, in turn a subset of the biosphere (Chapter 1, Figure 1.1). However, not only must environmental degradation be minimised or stopped, considerable ecological restoration is likely to be needed. This might require social transformations towards a restorative economy where investment in environmental restoration provides, among other benefits, the natural 'growth capital' for future sustainable and restorative industries. Ecotourism is a commonly cited example of an industry with a vested interest in biodiversity protection. Brunckhorst et al. (1997) describe investigations into other restorative industries in South Australia, where new markets are being developed for the meat, hides, and other products rendered from introduced goats and overabundant kangaroos that need culling to allow the land to recover from more than a century of overgrazing by introduced animals and pasture management.

Many of our political systems and institutions impede progress towards sustainability. For example the election cycle at any level of government (local, state, or national) promotes a short-term view and considers the electorate to have only short-term memories. Political parties develop their policies to get into power. Once in power, budget cycles are similarly short-term and often focused on the next election. The arbitrary nature of the political process is an obvious barrier to developing any long-term, adaptive strategies for land management. Political power structure is not in place long enough to adapt, and granting power to communities through bioregional frameworks is too often seen as a threat to centralised control.

Government and the Bureaucracy

There would appear to be little likelihood of coherent policies emerging from the traditional compartmentalised approach in which different departments, or different levels of government, each handle different, small parts of a problem. These narrow, short-term bureaucratic management approaches invariably turn into reactive treatments of symptoms rather than more effective and efficient, large-scale, long-term strategic actions guided by adaptive management. The nature of the legislative process and government tends to deliver highly codified laws and regulatory systems aimed at control rather than coordinated development of integrated programs and information sharing. Each of these pieces of policy is administered by a narrowly focused section of government. For example, the limited nature of endangered species and single species management programs, products of reductionist science, forge ahead apparently oblivious to the plethora of wider ecosystem or landscape and social management needs — externalised as someone else's responsibility.

Single agencies often have only a single focus. Even where areas of land have been designated for conservation or integrated resource use, resource development tends to be managed in accordance with government guidelines through a vast number of legislated instruments and the responsible agencies. Lack of coordination among agencies, often with competing mandates further exacerbates fragmentation of programs and dissatisfaction of the community and sectoral interests.

Cooperative trans-disciplinarity must be engendered, not only in science, but also across all land managers, government agencies, and citizens as a key part of strategic bioregional planning. A significant contribution of bioregional planning is matching context and scale. Working at a broader scale provides multiple options for resolving problems (without causing others) and achieving lasting results over wider areas with community support. Decision-makers working at a broader scale will not be limited to dealing with a single issue at a single site; instead, they can evaluate various components in the context (and influence) of other elements (Western *et al.* 1996, Brunckhorst *et al.* 1997, Brunckhorst 1998).

Institutionalised bureaucracies are becoming dysfunctional for other reasons. Any government official who has been involved in program delivery, administration of legislation, or perhaps more telling, sat in 'interdepartmental' meetings will know the sometimes considerable efforts that are taken to protect one's own territory, to avoid real cooperation even if it means duplicating programs or creating conflicting ones. Enormous effort goes toward competing against each other for financial gain or additional control. This even occurs between agencies or sections within the same department. Furthermore, departments and agencies often have overlapping jurisdictions, but different goals and legislated mandates causing them to work at cross-purposes and entrenching systems for mutual obstruction (Platt 1996).

Government departments and their officials do, however, have the opportunity to demonstrate leadership, openness in communication and build public trust by reducing protection of their narrowly focused territories of responsibility and by making public service a priority over organisational survival. Regionalisation of departments along the lines of bioregional planning and management frameworks to make them part of the local community and located together to work collaboratively might overcome some of these barriers (Saunders 1990, HoSCERA 1992, 1993). While some managers and officials might think them impossible or impractical, these solutions have started to evolve under critically pressured social, economic and ecological systems. In the Pacific Northwest, for example, the crisis of endangered owls and over-harvested old-growth forests forced intervention by the US President, who called for the creation of a bioregional solution that considered the long-term viability of communities, local industry, and the ecosystem.

Effectively managing and openly communicating the required internal organisational change will be essential to the successful reshaping of government institutions and bureaucracies. In order to restore trust between the general public and government departments, it will be necessary to shift away from structured, one-way approaches to public participation towards much more open and flexible approaches, which encourage a broad public discourse and dispersal of centralised authority (Stanley 1983, Orr 1992, Cortner and Shannon 1993).

There is also the need for fundamental change at two interrelated levels of government departments and agencies. First, at the inter-departmental (or inter-agency level), structural change is needed for agencies to be able to effectively deal with integrated approaches to the management of whole systems. This does not necessarily require the formation of mega-agencies, but rather a decentralised approach with closer links to regional environments and communities. Second, there is a requirement for internal organisational change in terms of institutional culture and management processes. It will be a challenge for those attuned to a single focus to adapt to the requirements for broad-scale, integrated ecosystem management. This will require the recognition and valuing of different styles of organisational learning (Argyris and Schon 1978, Carley and Christie 1992).

Institutionalised Research and Knowledge

The character of scientific research and academia also contribute obstacles. In contemporary western civilisation, nature and natural systems have been viewed as separate from humans, and traditional science reflects this view. The sense of community and belonging to a particular landscape is slowly being lost from many cultures (Knudtson and Suzuki 1992). Cartesian dualism in separating people from the environment also promotes compartmentalised and reductionist methodologies. While elucidating useful pure knowledge, these methods fragment our understanding of the functioning of whole complex systems and their results often cannot be applied in the broader spatio-temporal context that is required for successful ecosystem management. The separateness of the sciences is also an impediment to the implementation of regional scale, ecosystem management approaches. Again, this is neither simply a lack of knowledge of ecosystems, nor of the functioning of social or political systems, but a lack of inter-disciplinary research and development of applications of existing data across scales and jurisdictions. Consequently few studies exist to integrate data from several disciplines or to undertake trans-disciplinary research to measure policy successes and failures in natural resource management.

Universities and professional bodies are traditionally 'pigeon-holed' into disciplinary areas, but potentially have an important role to play in reshaping our institutions, policy makers and leaders of the future. Within academic institutions, the 'publish or perish' syndrome for tenure or promotion does not favour interdisciplinary (or long-term) studies, instead it encourages people to remain narrowly focused in one area of expertise. In turn, this promotes a lack of resource management understanding and organisational management skills of academics. For example, a consequence of these policies is reflected in genuine attempts to establish 'ecosystem management' or 'natural resource management' departments or schools in universities, which often end up staffed by pure biological science researchers. In contrast, they should have a compliment of social and ecological researchers, economists, policy (or institutional) analysts, managers and facilitators (or communicators). Their collective work, or rather influence, might be judged by the longevity of successful models of ecosystem management which they establish with local communities and government in regional areas.

What proportion of the tens of thousands of scientific papers published each year are actually used or applied to environmental resource and related human social problems? The availability and use of data and information to guide decision making by citizens, politicians, government and non-government organisations is another major impediment to establishing real 'on-ground' models or experimental management with local communities and government agencies as equal partners in pursuit of sustainability. Lack of full data and understanding must no longer be used as an excuse for inaction (Lovejoy 1995, Norton and Dovers 1996, Smythe et al. 1996). Obstacles to integration of information and communication across institutions, and to the public in general, are again attributable to inflexible or narrowly focused institutional cultures and jurisdictional barriers (Caldwell 1970, Saunders 1990, Brunckhorst and Bridgewater 1994, 1995, Hobbs and Humphries 1995). For example, often no one else is allowed access to the information an agency might compile, although the gathering of such was probably publicly funded. In addition, it is increasingly common for agencies to try to recover additional costs by a 'user pays' policy, effectively eliminating any incentive to use the data at all even if it might provide for better decision making.

Uncertainty permeates all policies and applications for ecologically sustainable resource use and conservation (Dovers et al. 1996). Natural resource issues, particularly at multiple scales of planning and management, are often characterised by high levels of complexity and low levels of certainty. Figure 4.1 illustrates a hierarchy of increasing integration and information exchange across disciplines and into management and decision making, while balancing lack of knowledge of the ecologically and socially complex systems through adaptive management. Prototype mechanisms for scientific, policy, institutional and management applications that transcend or remove impediments to broad-scale ecosystem management need to be developed (e.g., Brunckhorst et al. 1997). We need to elaborate trans-disciplinary methods to help us deal with uncertainty, manage risk and 'learn by doing' — experimentally and adaptively manage taking account of the bioregional context (Walters and Holling 1990, Forman 1995, Dovers et al. 1996). Adaptive management treats all policy applications and actions as experiments that are monitored and lessons are actively learnt and incorporated into future actions or the next implementation phase. In addition to being a useful institutional learning strategy, adaptive management is a valuable form of risk management when faced with a lack of information and uncertainty of potential reactions or surprises (Gunderson *et al.* 1995). Long enduring Common Property Regimes or Resource systems (CPRs) are community based collectives managing shared resources and shared property (ie, closed 'commons'; see Chapter 5), which have internalised risk management very successfully and self-regulated their resource use to match the social and ecological scales (Hanna *et al.* 1996, Berkes and Folke 1998). Regional landscape or bioregional applications of alternative futures analysis can also guide risk management and decision analysis for bioregional planning (Steinitz *et al.* 1996).

Enormous gains in efficiency will accrue through better communication, access to and use of information, freeing up institutionalised programs, and improving cross-jurisdictional responsibility for land-use management (Brunckhorst 1995, Brown and MacLeod 1996, Crance and Draper 1996). We need to experimentally develop the tools to facilitate institutional change in science policy, risk management, information use policy, administrative policy, and public consultative policies. Such real-life adaptive management is discussed in subsequent chapters.

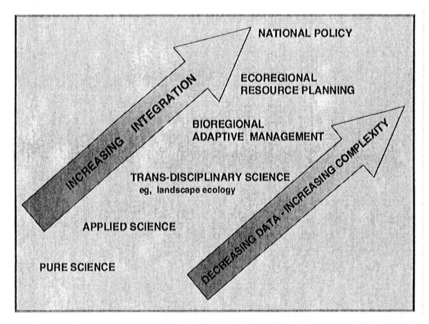

Figure 4.1. Balancing the uncertainty of ecological systems by increasing integration and information use through flexible planning and adaptive management.

Despite the state of our current institutions, flexible and adaptable institutions have the potential to play a major role in bioregional planning and management because they can help identify common values among citizen, government and corporate interests across the multiple scales necessary for ecological sustainability (Smil 1993, Norton and Dovers 1996, Coleman 1996, Platt 1996). Paul Hawken (1993: 203) explains the required paradigmatic shift in the following way:

> ... a critical basis for change and consensus is to find a way to introduce and discuss ecological principles in a manner that draws people together, rather than repelling or deterring them. This step is crucial, because within ecological principles reside not only the problems and challenges that face us, but also the solutions that can be used to transform our economy and society.

Hawken 1993: 203.

Some possible elements of an inclusive approach to surmounting institutional barriers are listed in Box 4.1. These consensual approaches might be considered when working towards improved operation among various institutions, and cooperative planning and management within an operational bioregion. They provide a starting point for designing a practical audit of social and institutional capacity within a bioregional framework.

NEW DIMENSIONS: SOCIAL FUNCTIONS, RESOURCE GOVERNANCE AND BIOREGIONS

Increasing evidence shows that the biosphere is not infinitely adaptable to human perturbations (Brunckhorst 1998). Similarly, we are now beginning to understand that society and its institutions may be infinitely adaptable in theory, but not in practice. It remains to be seen if the social transformations towards a sustainable future are of the order to shift all sectoral institutions to such a long-term commitment. Sustainability at the temporal scale of future generations requires long-term vision and social flexibility. It also requires strategic integrated planning, policy development and implementation across traditional institutional boundaries. Policy and management responses to the challenges of sustainability will need systems approaches that reflect the complexity of the natural world and the cultural values associated with it (Berkes and Folke 1998). The future role of policy and administration at all levels of government (as well as the private sector) will be critically important to how sustainable our future might turn out to be.

Box 4.1 Practical Institutional Analysis: Examining Solutions

A problem analysis approach to identifying institutional issues and solutions could be structured in the following way (with community, local government and land management agencies as equal partners):

♦ Examine alternative organisational arrangements for collaborative management, ownership and responsibility to accomplish ecosystem management goals.

♦ Develop research protocols, methods and theoretical bases for problem solving of institutional, cultural and social barriers to integrated resource management

♦ Examine communication relationships between agencies and rural landholders and/or community (including information access, technology transfer and adoption)

♦ Analyse the extent to which existing laws, policies and regulations may constrain or aid applications of landscape ecosystem management approaches

♦ Examine rural community applications of regional ecosystem management and difficulties encountered (eg, local agencies, Landcare groups, catchment management groups).

♦ Examine the potential of various forms of partnership models within and across bioregions (eg, Community Land-Management Trusts; Community Commons for adaptive management)

♦ Examine rural community perceptions of government or other institutional regulations and programs for natural resource management

♦ Assess the role of local government in rural applications of regional environmental planning and management

♦ Examine government agency arrangements for implementing programs.

♦ Assess existing and novel tools for cross-jurisdictional land management.

♦ Identify causes of poor relationships between agency cultures and programs, and community groups; also examine issues effecting 'group overload', cynicism, efficiency and effective implementation of programs.

♦ Experimentally develop ('learning by doing') innovative mechanisms to breakdown barriers to communication and adoption of integrated (bioregional) resource management approaches in rural and allied industries.

♦ Identify improvements to the organisational and institutional structures and practices, policies and cultures of government agencies.

♦ Synthesise methods and tools to improve processes and structures of citizen led action to accomplish regional ecosystem management goals.

The radical individualism such as that of the 18th and 19th century frontier societies in Australia and North America, and the association between land ownership and civil liberty (Bromley 1982), causes no problems as long as ecosystems are insulating the activities of individuals from each other. However, as soon as the evolution of the landscape under its regime of individualist resource use results in the loss of this ecological insulation and harmful externalities begin to be transmitted by ecosystems, the need for resource governance arises.

Ian Reeve (1998: 6)

Clearly, human use of natural resources has exceeded the bounds of ecological insulation, as Reeve describes above. Undoubtedly, future sustainability will depend on a system of resource governance that mediates the relationship between society (including the economy) and the biosphere in which it is nested. Studies of regional ecology must therefore address not only bio-geo-chemical relationships, but also institutional functions that ultimately have ecological effects leading to social and economic consequences. This might best be accomplished if social science and policy studies are conducted in tandem with large-scale ecological research. The information generated from policy studies can then be incorporated into other systems models of the interactions among socio-economics, policy decisions and ecosystem functions (Bird 1987, Schlager and Ostrom 1992, Costanza 1993, Samson and Knopf 1996, Brown and Macleod 1996, Smythe *et al.* 1996). Such integrated efforts will be critically important to identifying key issues and related scientific questions, as well as adapting management strategies, institutions and citizenry led civic governance (Ostrom 1990, Armitage 1995, Weeks 1996, Shannon 1998).

Institutional Adaptation for Sustainable Resource Governance

The extent to which communities and institutions are able to adapt to a system of ecologically sustainable resource governance will determine whether the functioning of the economy and actions of people sustain or erode the natural processes on which society relies (see Ostrom 1990, Young 1992, Bromley 1991, 1992, De Leo and Levin 1997). While some institutional adaptation has occurred towards sustainable resource governance (particularly in the development of community based resource management), the pace of institutional adaptation falls far short of what is needed to overcome the rate of land degradation that has occurred in the last few decades (Reeve 1997). There is an urgent need, particularly in rural areas, to increase the pace of institutional adaptation for sustainable resource governance while there is still capacity in the ecosystem to recover. Too often action is seen as unnecessary, and change is delayed until the ecosystem is so badly disrupted that few options remain for the people who live there. We therefore need some rationale to develop resource governance that make sense in terms of sustaining ecosystem function and community function across landscapes, with which the citizenry feel they can identify (Schaaf T. 1995, Brunckhorst 1995, 1998, Schoonmaker *et al.* 1996, Walton and Bridgewater 1996).

Unfortunately, little recognition has been given to the need for resource governance systems to be crafted to fit both the biophysical and socio-economic contexts within which they must function. The current system of governance characterised by political expedience and bureaucratic inertia favours the modification of existing institutional forms rather than developing new ones (Caldwell 1970, Norton and Dovers 1996, Reeve 1996, 1997).

Institutional cultural change and capacity building towards new organisational forms for sustainable resource governance will require several key elements, including (after Brunckhorst 1995, 1998, Reeve 1997, 1998, Brunckhorst and Rollings 1999, Rollings and Brunckhorst 1999):

- spatial information of social and ecological functions;
- understanding (social and ecological) influence functions on components across landscapes;
- coordinated resource governance policy;
- flexible adaptation by community, civic and institutional elements; and
- enforcement by community established governance.

Integrated social and ecological mapping

To be effective in achieving sustainable resource use, resource governance systems should reflect the character and dynamics of the ecosystems involved, and the social, cultural and institutional norms of the society to which resource users belong (Brunckhorst 1995, Brunckhorst and Bridgewater 1995). Mapping the ecological and social functional processes and their influence on the landscape will help decision-makers understand the consequences of their choices (Brunckhorst 1998, Rollings and Brunckhorst 1999). Such mapping would help illustrate where resources are a part of broader scale systems, and would suggest an operational 'nesting' where the scale of governance is matched to the scale of the resource, ecosystem function and associated externalities — the essence of adaptive management within a strategic bioregional framework (e.g., Walters 1986, Walters and Holling 1990, Gunderson *et al.* 1995, Johnson *et al.* 1999).

Despite the various difficulties described, it now should be possible to bring together three types of spatially distributed information that are fundamental to the design and building of more ecologically sustaining, resource governance systems. These are:

1. Institutional mapping techniques;
2. The distribution of social, environmental and political values held by those with interest in particular resources; and
3. Functional, ecological-connectivity between landscape components.

In Australia, the USA, Canada and Europe, geographic information systems and techniques that detail biophysical characteristics are increasingly common (Bailey *et al*. 1985, Omernik 1987, Thackway and Cresswell 1993, Brunckhorst *et al*. 1994, Bunce *et al*. 1996). The use of such systems for institutional mapping appears to have been overlooked. This might be due to the natural evolution of spatial information systems. Over the past 10 years many organisations have been involved in massive data collection projects. Extensive databases have, and are continuing, to be built, yet very little attention has been paid to database use, user access and the development of graphic visualisation (Rollings 1996). However mapping of institutions and the influence of organisational entities on landscape components can be mapped (Rollings and Brunckhorst 1999). Details such as constraints, opportunities and responsibilities that pertain to land uses on each component, as a consequence of the bodies of common law, statute law and associated scheduled regulations administered by various government agencies, will be useful in defining new governance systems (Reeve 1997, Brunckhorst 1998, Brunckhorst and Rollings 1999,).

The second type of spatial information required is the distribution, magnitude and direction of social, environmental and political values held by those parties with interest in particular resources. Further understanding of these values, together with various options in framing resource issues, is essential in determining to what extent resource governance can depend on social and cultural institutions to provide monitoring and enforcement services; and to what extent these services may have to be established by the state or other institutions at the regional level (Schlager and Ostrom 1992, Reeve 1992, 1997, Black and Reeve 1993, Berkes and Folke 1998).

The third essential spatial information required for the design of resource governance systems is the extent of functional, ecological connectivity between landscape components.

In attempting to draw these three kinds of spatial attributes together, Rollings and Brunckhorst (1999) refer to the 'Influence Functions' of ecological and social components. The spatial influence of ecological and social functions can be mapped, as a 3-dimensional 'Influence Surface' (Figure 4.2). A combined influence surface is generated and pattern analysis can be employed to elucidate landscape scale management zones, a bioregional framework, that best match the scale of ecological and social influences.

Such influence mapping has the potential to reflect the involvement of citizens, local governments and agencies so that institutional learning and adaptation are a mutually inclusive (and measurable) part of the entire adaptive program of management. A characteristic spatial context for sustainable resource management and options for resource governance for each bioregional management framework can then be identified. This spatial framework can be used to guide the design of resource governance systems that consider influences and sustain the functioning of ecological processes and services at a bioregional scale. A bioregional framework elucidated by this methodology might also provide the systems context for social and institutional engagement in adaptive management that is necessary, but generally lacking in current resource management (McLain and Lee 1996).

A bioregional framework provides a mechanism for integration of all levels of social organisation for long term sustainability. The objective for bioregional planning and management is to facilitate the emergence of culturally appropriate local and regional systems of resource governance and associated flexible and adaptive institutions. These must match resource access to the bioregional capacity to provide resources and ecosystem services.

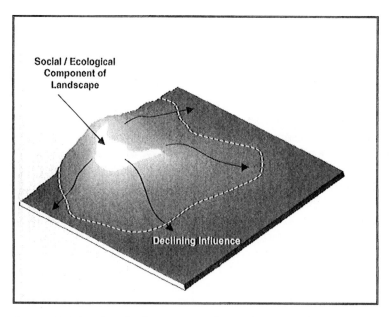

Figure 4.2. A hypothetical *Influence Function* illustrated as a three dimensional surface (after Rollings and Brunckhorst 1999). The integration of social and ecological influences, their effect on each other, and decline of their influence across regional landscapes can guide analysis of more appropriate bioregional context (dotted line) to adjust institutional arrangements for resource governance.

CHAPTER 5

THE ROLE OF GOVERNMENT, PRIVATE INDIVIDUALS AND THE PRIVATE SECTOR

Although industry is accustomed to dealing with broad environmental concerns (such as global warming and acid rain), the biodiversity issue invokes hemisphere-wide, regional, local, and site-specific concerns all at the same time.

Coleman 1996: 815

William Coleman, a researcher in the environment group of the Electric Power Research Institute in California, emphasises both the imperatives and the capacities of industry to engage with and contribute to multiple scales of resource and biodiversity management. Through the examination of the issues of ecosystem health, ecosystem integrity and human needs, he concludes that industry and the corporate sector can help guide the regional ecosystem management vision by contributing practical viewpoints and abilities and encouraging a relevant agenda of applied research, policy and management (Coleman 1996).

In Europe, the USA and Australia, many companies are now taking environmental matters seriously. To some it is a matter of toeing the line of the law and avoiding litigation, because in these countries, directors (at Board of Directors level) may be liable for pollution or environmental degradation (Chester and Rowley 1992). Many companies, however, now accept that corporate citizenship involves not only environmental responsibility in their activities, but the sharing of knowledge, capacities and resources of the company. For example, many mining companies (some perhaps to improve their 'public image') sponsor and engage in ecological restoration projects with community groups, government or environmental non-government organisations (NGOs). Many companies especially in the USA, now have their own philanthropic trust funds, and various of these give priority to sustainable community development initiatives including environmental restoration.

This chapter examines some emerging novel forms of integrated public, private and community approaches that are useful in building practical bioregional planning and management models for the future. The following chapter describes some case studies that illustrate some elements and principles discussed below.

MANAGING COMPLEX ECOLOGICAL AND SOCIAL SYSTEMS

As society struggles to come to grips with increasing degradation of the land, its resources and faltering ecosystems, all governments are realising their limited capacities to assist social change towards a sustainable future. The success of some on-ground activities of various community-based movements throughout the world has also contributed to public debate on the appropriate responses of government.

The nature of the huge task of environmental management and repair means that traditional approaches and the already stretched resources of the public sector, while essential, cannot do the job alone. It is increasingly necessary to entwine strategies for ecologically sustainable development and conservation across public (government) institutional management frameworks as well as across the corporate sector and traditional forms of private land management and use. In developed countries, citizens generally consider that government should have all the means to deal with any problem, whether environmental, social or economic. While governments should contribute more than they do at present to environmental concerns, it is now becoming apparent that they do not have all the funds, expertise and various other tools and capacities that are required to tackle these issues. As noted in the previous chapter, our current forms of public sector organisation have limited capabilities to deal effectively with the scale, complexity and inter-relatedness of environmental problems for long term sustainability. Government agencies and bureaucracies tend to lack the flexibility required to adapt to or engage in more integrated on-ground models with local people, and a focus on sustainability has been lacking in many community development initiatives.

Society like ecosystem is a nesting of processes at multiple scales and all levels of organisation are reflected in every geographic place (Chapters 2 and 3). In bioregional design, we need to work from 'place' to integrate the multiple capacities of social systems. A bioregional context matching social processes of organisation with functional processes of regional landscape ecosystems helps draw together common values for the future. The bioregion becomes the 'Place of Integration' (chapter 3). With the inherently dynamic nature of society, novel public-private partnerships, and new organisational forms and structures can evolve to deal with previously intractable issues (see Brunckhorst *et al.* 1997, Meidinger 1998, Johnson *et al* 1999.).

The private sector, regional communities, community interest groups, and individual citizens all have resources and capabilities to contribute. Engaging in partnerships and networks to build these capacities and harness them requires considerable facilitation and an effort by all parties. Equal partnerships between government, the private sector and local communities are therefore an essential requirement for a sustainable future. In partnership with government, rural communities can contribute their time, skills, and knowledge of local conditions to develop experimental approaches to conservation, sustainable land uses and landscape recovery. A partnership approach of weaving sectoral issues and interests together within the holistic framework of a bioregion serves to align, integrate and coordinate the programs and services associated with those sectors. I like to think of this strategic capacity building approach as 'bottom-up, top-down and sideways-in'. Bottom-up refers to the resources, talents and time of people and interest groups in the local community, including the local civic or municipal capacities and support. Top-down is generally seen as the coordination, funding and professional capacities of national or state governments and their agencies (this might include government research agencies and universities). Sideways-in capacities and resources can be important in assisting local communities with funds, professional expertise and corporate or private sector support coming into communities from within or outside of the region. It reflects some of the principles of 'action-centred networking' described by Carley and Christie (1992).

Citizenry led community participation

The average citizen is typically on the fringe of environmental decision making, having neither the power nor the resources to make or influence decisions that affect them. Consultation processes where members of the public put forward their views are seldom satisfying for the decision-makers or the public. Too often, decisions have already been made and plans developed before the consultation process, leaving citizen input as little more than a footnote to the process. Citizens may resort to administrative and legal redress mechanisms for their grievances, which is costly and seldom effective. Such outcomes, in turn, further direct resources away from operational activity and only serve to build tense relationships between the public, the knowledge holders and the decision-makers.

Frustration is not limited to the general public. Decision makers in government and business are often frustrated by the inability of existing policy and decision-making processes to reach timely and effective outcomes. Similarly, researchers, teachers and extension officers are frustrated in seeing information under-utilised due to ineffective communication links. Increasingly, government officers and decision-makers (who it should be remembered are part of the local community) share a common desire for a pro-active, alternative decision-making process which avoids the harmful conflicts of many existing models (see Shannon 1992, 1998, Maguire and Boiney 1994, Reid and Murphy 1995, Samson and Knopf 1996).

Equalising all public, private and community interests through partnerships focussed on common values and concerns is not impossible (see Schaaf 1995, Western *et al.* 1996, Brunckhorst *et al.* 1997). If agencies can collectively see the benefits, are willing to give up some control, empower local people with real responsibility, support them and don't desert them, and engage with local communities and civic leaders in equal partnership, real progress can be made. Planning at the bioregional level can become an inter-agency initiative with substantial public involvement. For example, one integrative tool is the use of inter-agency 'Bioregional Facilitators' to link site specific community actions as well as agency activity to collectively contribute to broader scale ecosystem management goals. While conforming to higher-level plans (ecoregional and national/subcontinental) and other policy domains, local bioregional resource management plans can establish strategic objectives in a smaller area in order to provide specific direction for operational activities. Such plans can be used to resolve conflicts for areas such as watersheds, transport corridors, grazing and agriculture, recreation and conservation areas (Maguire and Boiney 1994). They can cover areas as large as several hundred thousand hectares or as small as a stream of a sub-catchment draining a few square kilometres. The use of bioregional planning as a tool to inform and guide decision-making, with a series of nested plans moving from broader to more specific levels of detail, can assist in moving towards an ecosystem-based management focus within and across communities and breaking down institutional barriers.

Significant steps must then be taken to broaden decision-making to include the full range of stakeholders One of the most significant positive changes emerging in resource governance is the move from representative democracy towards participatory democracy. As outlined above, public demand for participation has been motivated by frustration with the way government goes about making decisions and doing business. There has been the appearance of leaving out some parts of the community and favouring the powerful, the economically strong or merely the loudest, acting without consideration of all available information, and not giving enough weight to certain considerations such as ecosystem integrity. Options that involve a basic change in the status quo have not always been considered. Options have been rejected before evaluation, generally for reasons that are not valid, such as pressure from particular interests or the fear of losing control.

Responding to public dissatisfaction, and recognising that decisions incorporating various different interests are more stable and enduring, many government agencies have now incorporated extensive public involvement into decision-making processes related to areas of public concern. It can well be argued that this needs to be extended to the devolution of real responsibility back to local people in partnership with local governments and local government agencies. Where this has happened, the outcome has been real social and institutional adaptation, in turn resulting in the integration and better coordination of resource management efforts (e.g., Heinen 1995, Western *et al.* eds 1996, Brunckhorst *et al.* 1997, Berkes and Folke 1998).

Active-adaptive 'learning-by-doing'

Fundamentally, institutional evolution towards a culture that can encourage and partake of integrated models requires a new definition of management — replacing the idea of control by a few people with that of negotiation and organisational learning. Hence, management becomes teamwork (by partners) based on a continually evolving accord on the values associated with ecologically sustainable development (Carley and Christie 1992). Equally, facilitation of social change towards the emergence of new 'behavioural norms', attitudes, land management techniques and cooperation for future sustainability is best achieved through real 'on-ground' engagement with various processes and projects.

Consider these three generalised, but typical approaches to the management of natural resources, ecosystems and landscapes.

The first is referred to as the 'deferred action' method. As implied, this approach says management should not proceed until ecosystems, habitats and their interrelationships are fully understood. While entrenched in many institutional cultures, deferred action is untenable if we are committed to maintaining social quality and biodiversity because such ultimate knowledge can never be achieved. Neither society nor biodiversity can afford to wait any longer to learn to live together sustainably. Furthermore, this approach tends to overlook important feedback processes, which are themselves generated by the interdependence or connectivity of ecological and social systems across landscapes (Heinen 1995, Lovejoy 1995, Brunckhorst *et al.* 1997).

A second approach, 'passive adaptive' management, suggests that management proceeds on a basis of the 'best understanding' of the system using reactive strategies given that mistakes can be expected. Experience gained from mistakes can be used to improve the management model of the system. This approach is useful, but unfortunately it tends to be implemented too late and as large reactions when compound errors become un-manageable. Managers cannot afford to make mistakes when the system they manage has lost its resilience. Such is the case with many endangered species recovery programs, implemented at the brink of extinction when any mistake carries enormous risk.

The third method, termed the 'active adaptive approach' (active 'experimental management') considers management actions as deliberate experiments which are designed to both manage effectively and to generate better information for long-term management with the goal being long term sustainability (Walters and Holling 1990, Carley and Christie 1992). In effect, this method becomes a process of 'learning-by-doing' (or 'active-learning'). The active adaptive approach is also the most flexible in that varying economic and social demands on management will also contribute to a changing definition of 'on-ground' sustainability. Hence, an active adaptive approach is required to match the dynamism of a biophysical, economic and social system that continually requires readjustment and the setting of new management targets. This is the essence of adaptive management espoused by Walters (1986) and, Holling and Walters (1990), but emphasises the 'on-the-job' active learning part of the process. In addition to the monitoring-feedback-adapt management cycle, action-learning contributes increased data and understanding, and increased communication at a local community level where it is most needed (see Argyris and Schon 1978). A monitoring capability is an essential ingredient of this approach and can easily be incorporated into a partnership between agency and community for monitoring ecological reference sites (e.g., Burnside and Chamala 1994, Schriever and Birch 1995). Learning-by-doing (the active-adaptive approach) is the most appropriate for landscape recovery and, integrated bioregional planning and management implemented by the community and partners (government agencies, local government, public and private sectors, and specific 'outside' individual capacities).

Carley and Christie (1992) describe an 'action-centred network' participative-design approach so that socially meaningful action and change grow from a blending of experiential learning with other kinds of knowledge, within a 'big picture' context such as a biocultural landscape or bioregion. Figure 5.1 outlines the basic components of action-centred networking (after Carley and Christie 1992). An example of this approach is given in the Biosphere Reserve case studies in the following chapter; further examples can be found in the book edited by David Western and colleagues (Western *et al.* 1996).

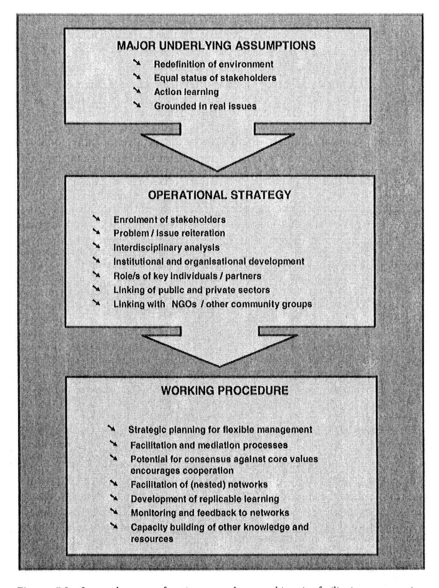

Figure 5.1. Some elements of action-centred networking in facilitating community-government and public-private partnerships (after Carley and Christie 1992).

The challenges of cross-jurisdictional, sustainable ecosystem management imply networked structures of public, private and community partnerships, generally with a focus on the local landscapes — the place of integration and implementation. Errol Meidinger (1997, 1998) refers to these primarily horizontal, institutional forms as 'Networked Order'.

> *The key characteristics of networked order are the use of horizontal alliances and partnerships to achieve coordinated action, a heavy reliance on communication and information flow, and an emphasis on flexibility and adaptation. … If networked structures aiding cross-boundary stewardship are to flourish, key elements of existing structures will have to change.*
>
> Meidinger (1998: 98–99)

Developing networks of partnerships can be an effective tool at regional and local levels for developing a strategic approach to integrative management. This will be further enriched by facilitating the emergence of an action-learning culture within the organisation and with partners. Within a bioregional framework, these processes working jointly with an appropriate legislative framework that validates integrative approaches by government agencies, can build strong and lasting community-government-private sector partnerships working towards a sustainable future.

ENDURING COMMON PROPERTY RESOURCE INSTITUTIONS

> *Communal tenure … promotes both general access to and optimum production from certain types of resources while enjoining on the entire community the conservation measures necessary to protect these resources from destruction.*
>
> Netting 1976: 145

Bioregional planning frameworks could help facilitate the emergence of contemporary, culturally appropriate local systems of resource governance, nesting within the regional context. These must match access to natural resource capacity for production and ecosystem services across local to regional scales. Flexible and adaptable institutions for governance of common pool resources are fundamentally important for sustainable land use management. They can help identify common values among citizen, government and corporate interests across the multiple scales necessary for ecological sustainability.

Common pool resources are defined as a class of resources for which exclusion is difficult and joint-use involves subtractibility (Berkes 1989). Most renewable natural resources fall within this definition. There are two fundamental problems that arise from the basic characteristics of all such resources. First, how to control access to the resource — the exclusion problem, which may lead to privatisation and then increasing externalisation of degradation and central regulation. Second, how to institute rules among users to solve the potential divergence between individual and collective rationality — the subtractibility problem of unsustainable harvest.

One theory of common pool resource systems is that users were always trapped in an inexorable 'Tragedy of the Commons', (Hardin 1968), because more users would simply introduce more cattle to graze (or other resource subtraction). Many studies, especially since the mid 1980s, have shown Hardin's theory usually only applies to open-access commons (see Bromley 1992, Hanna *et al.* 1996). If the resource is freely open to access by any user, a tragedy of the commons does eventually follow. More often, however, resources used collectively by rural communities are not open-access but are under communal property rights arrangements (Common Property Regimes — CPRs) with rules regarding access and joint use (Ostrom 1990, McKean 1992a, Berkes and Folke 1998). An examination of enduring commons reveals these common property management institutions — despite intensive use and a high degree of unpredictability — have sustained their natural resource base over the centuries. Institutions that have built-in adaptiveness and resilience are capable of responding to and managing processes, functions, dynamics and changes in a fashion that contributes to ecosystems resilience. Many of these common-property institutions have a proven track record that extends over long periods and generally consist of self-governing associations of local users managing common property resources or 'commons' (Ostrom 1990, Bromley 1991, 1992, Keohane and Ostrom 1995, Hanna *et al.* 1996, Berkes and Folke 1998).

Thirsk (1964) identifies four key attributes defining the core dimensions of common field agriculture. First, the holdings of individual cultivators comprising many separate parcels scattered among unenclosed common fields termed 'strips in the arable' (Dahlman 1980). Second, after the harvest, and usually during fallow years, these common-fields revert from private farmland to communal pasture ground, as all villagers exercise their customary right to graze their animals on the herbage temporarily available on the arable land and was termed 'common of shack'. Third, the land that was unsuitable for cropping, termed 'common waste', was utilised for common grazing. Finally, regulation and supervision of the entire system was provided by an 'assembly of cultivators' or 'communal regulation' (Dahlman 1980). There is historical evidence that agricultural villages with common pasturages of this type existed in many other places besides England and Europe, including Africa, Asia, India, and Central and South America. Nomadic pastoralists in Africa still support themselves by grazing livestock in common pasturages. In the great majority of these cases thoughtful restrictions on access and intensity of use have averted the tragedy of the common by these community groups (Gardner and Stern 1996).

Mountain commons in both Switzerland and Japan have been sustained over centuries while being used intensively. On February 1, 1483 the Swiss village of Törbel formalised in writing a charter governing the management of the summer alpine meadows which were grazed as a common resource (actually, some evidence of this commons dates back as early as 1224). The traditional Commons Lands (Iraichi) in Japan came into being between the thirteenth and sixteenth centuries, though the tradition of the common may have begun more than a thousand years earlier (McKean 1992b). As late as the 1950s there were many expanses of common land in Japan still being managed collectively without ecological destruction despite the infusion of industrial wealth into rural Japan. Japanese villages obviously altered the landscape of the commons from its natural state, but they also clearly operated their commons according to the principle of sustainable yield so as not to degrade it as a productive resource.

Eighty-four irrigators served by the Banecher River and Faitanar canals in Valencia, Spain gathered to sign their formal articles of association on May 29, 1435. However, many of the rules regarding distribution of water within the common property institution, carried into medieval and modern practice were probably developed some 1000 years prior to the recapture of Valencia from the Muslims in 1238 (Ostrom 1990). Keeping order and maintaining large-scale irrigation works in the difficult terrain of Spain has been a similarly remarkable achievement. That record has not been matched by most of the irrigation systems constructed around the world in the past 50 years.

An important characteristic of enduring, self-governing commons is that they all face uncertain and complex environments. In contrast to the uncertainty of these environments, the populations at these locations have remained stable over long periods of time — members have shared a past and expect to share a future. The comprehensive study Ostrom (1990) identified the following eight similarities among enduring, self-governing common property resource (CPR) institutions and more recent case studies (e.g., McKean 1992a, Keohane and Ostrom 1995, Hanna et al. 1996, Berkes and Folke 1998) appear to confirm these principles.

1. Clearly defined boundaries. Individuals or households who have rights to withdraw resource units from the commons must be clearly defined, as must the boundaries of the commons itself.
2. Congruence between appropriation and provision rules and local conditions — appropriation rules restricting time, place, technology, and/or quantity of resource units are related to local conditions and to provision rules requiring labour, material, and/or money.
3. Collective choice arrangements — most individuals affected by the operational rules can participate in modifying the operational rules.
4. Monitoring — monitors, who actively audit commons condition and appropriator behaviour, are accountable to the appropriators or are the appropriators
5. Graduated sanctions — appropriators who violate operational rules are likely to be imposed with graduated sanctions (depending on the seriousness and context of the offence) by other appropriators, and/or by officials accountable to these appropriators.
6. Conflict resolution mechanisms — appropriators and their officials have rapid access to low cost local arenas to resolve conflicts among appropriators or between appropriators and officials.
7. Minimal recognition of rights to organise — the rights of appropriators to devise their own institutions are not challenged by external governmental authorities.
8. Nested enterprises — appropriation, monitoring, enforcement, conflict resolution, and governance activities are organised in multiple layers of nested enterprises (a particular feature of CPR's that are a part of larger systems).

It is clear from the foregoing discussion in this Chapter that there is an urgent need to design institutions that safeguard the dynamic capacity of ecological and resource production systems. Resource and ecosystem management is necessary but it requires fundamentally different approaches, not mere tinkering with current models and practices. One way of rethinking resource management social science will be through a focus on property rights institutions and in particular common-property systems. Modern, contemporary CPRs need to be developed as experimental models (Hanna *et al.* 1996, McKean 1997).

Adoption and adaptation of an enduring CPR planning and management approach is one of the challenges being undertaken by *Ecologically Restorative Industries* (ERI) on the New England Tablelands of Australia. The experimental model provides the opportunity for a CPR collective incorporating a group of graziers, who together own (free-hold tenure) and have a long-term interest in a sub-catchment. They have collectively agreed to work and learn together how to operate a CPR system (Coop and Brunckhorst 1999). Together with capacity building support of an accountant, lawyer and staff of the UNESCO Institute for Bioregional Resource Management (University of New England), the landholders are assessing a variety of options. Firstly, for the necessary structures for operational as well as insurance and other requirements (e.g., Co-Operative, Unit Trust, Incorporated Association or Company) and it would appear that several will be needed linked to each other. Secondly, a number of formulae are being discussed for sharing of resources, areas, labour, infrastructure and profits relative to their contributions. Thirdly, the relative make-up of the combined herd and opportunities for ecological restoration of the sub-catchment coupled with new diversifications that can be pursued using the additional labour and professional capacities that will be generated (Coop and Brunckhorst 1999). Development of this contemporary CPR as an experimental model in a industrialised federated nation is proving to be quite a challenge and it will necessarily be a long term process. It has great potential, however, to deal with a range of rural issues and as a potential vehicle demonstrating institutional transformation and new forms of resource management towards enduring ecological and social systems at a landscape level.

Linked social-ecological systems, such as these enduring commons, have developed the ability to respond to changes and to adapt in an active way because such adaptations were key to survival. There is increasing evidence that local-level institutions learn and develop the capability to respond to environmental feedbacks faster than do centralised agencies. Learning from local social-ecological systems and combining insights gained in adaptive management in western science may counteract many of the prevailing crises of conventional resource management. In addition the nested hierarchy of community-based action and lessons from institutions with such enduring resilience might be applicable nested within the bioregions, which in turn, are nested in ecoregions and so on up to the level of the biosphere (Chapter 2).

PART III
EFFECTING INTEGRATION, COORDINATION AND COOPERATION

CHAPTER 6

Biosphere Reserve Case Studies
Of Bioregional Management

Biosphere reserves offer such a model. Rather than becoming islands in an increasingly impoverished and chaotic world, they can become theatres for reconciling people and nature; they can demonstrate how to overcome the problems of the sectoral nature of our institutions.

Seville Strategy (UNESCO 1995)

The case studies briefly outlined in this chapter illustrate many of the principles for bioregional resource planning and management, community and public-private capacity building and multi-scale, multi-level integration at landscape regional scales. Though they are all quite different, the examples just happen to be Biosphere Reserves as well. It might be useful, therefore to quickly describe the current evolution of this UNESCO program.

The UNESCO Man and the Biosphere (MAB), biosphere reserve program is actually one form of bioregional planning that has long proposed such regional-landscape scale, integrated 'on-ground' models be developed with local communities (Batisse 1982, 1990, 1996, Dyer and Holland 1991, Castaneda 1993, Brunckhorst and Bridgewater 1994, Brunckhorst *et al.* 1997). The UNESCO program provides an integrative tool for managing whole landscape systems, including their socio-economic features. It unites conservation and sustainable development across the landscape; provides a strategic framework for land use management across jurisdictions — coupled to monitoring sites across the landscape and, globally, to the international network of biosphere reserves.

At an international level, for example, the Mediterranean Blue Plan is an innovative, ecoregional (level II/III integration, see Chapter 2) approach to international land-sea management having a variety of socio-economic and urbanisation issues (see Batisse 1996). The plan is endeavouring to assess urban, agricultural and natural zones around the Mediterranean coast. It is examining the potential effects of development and conservation under several future scenarios. Estimates of possible changes wrought by these futures should provide guidance in seeking international coordination of policy and planning instruments.

The UNESCO is also looking to the future and pursuing elaboration of a variety of bioregional planning and management tools and approaches that might be incorporated into the MAB program as elaborated by the IUCN-UNESCO *Montreal Protocol* of 1996. Partnerships are being developed to focus interdisciplinary research integrated with community and civic action.

BIOSPHERE RESERVES: CONCEPTS AND CONFUSION

The seminal meeting for what would become the 'Man and the Biosphere' (MAB) biosphere reserve program was held at UNESCO House in Paris in 1968. The Biosphere Reserve program began in earnest with the first meeting of the MAB International Co-ordinating Council in 1971.

The international network of biosphere reserves was proposed to protect the world's major biomes or ecological units. By the time the 'Minsk' Action Plan for Biosphere Reserves (UNESCO 1984) was produced, the program was already visionary; aiming to reconcile utilisation of natural resources with long term protection through an interdisciplinary approach to sustaining nature and society (Batisse 1982, 1993, UNESCO 1984, 1995). Over 200 Biosphere Reserves had been nominated by 1984. There are now 330 Biosphere Reserves in 125 participating nations. The international network also provided a unique set of sites and opportunities for long term monitoring, research and communication into the ecological, social and economic aspects of conservation and sustainable development.

Its mission now focuses on the need to reconcile the utilisation of natural resources with long term protection of biodiversity through an interdisciplinary approach to sustaining nature and society.

The UNESCO Biosphere Reserve program was reviewed at an international conference in Spain in 1995. More than 500 delegates from more than 100 countries and 300 biosphere reserves attended. In conclusion, 'Vision from Seville' noted that biosphere reserves should 'preserve and generate natural and cultural values through management that is scientifically correct, culturally creative and operationally sustainable' (UNESCO 1995). The resultant *Seville Strategy* for the development and application of Biosphere Reserves into the next century encourages the elaboration of bioregional approaches to their planning and management. It highlights the importance of biosphere reserves as models for land management and experimental approaches to sustainable development (UNESCO 1995), including:

- Involvement of stakeholders in decision making and responsibility, especially where there are critical interactions between humans and their environment; for example, across peri-urban areas, degraded rural areas, coastal zones and wetlands.
- Identification of incompatibilities across areas of different logistical function such as conservation and sustainable use and the development of mechanisms, including conflict resolution, to ensure appropriate balances are maintained.
- Integration into regional planning at larger scales together with monitoring of indicators for sustainability of various natural resources uses at such scales.
- Mobilisation of private funds and capacity building partnerships from business, industry, foundations and NGOs.
- Definition of training needs and other requirements for design and implementation; especially, across socio-cultural conditions, and for mediation and co-operative resource management in a landscape context.

The outcomes from Seville reinforced the biosphere reserve model as fundamentally concerned with whole of landscape processes, whether inside or outside of protected areas, across a variety of land tenures and uses, and socio-cultural spheres of operation (Dyer and Holland 1991, Brunckhorst and Bridgewater 1994). They aim to sustain the biodiversity and productive capacity on a regional scale that is appropriate to the ecological processes and human use and cultural identity within that landscape. Hence, they are vehicles for managing the social, cultural and institutional change and capacity building which is required to deal with the future sustenance of the biosphere and humanity.

The MAB program provides a multiple tool box to explore new methods for planning and practising sustainable resource management which is integrated with conservation activities. A Biosphere Reserve gives local communities new responsibilities for their own sustainable future while providing a thread to re-sew peoples' identity to the landscape. This contrasts with managing their own 'patch' in isolation and/or being excluded from ownership and responsibility for managing nearby public land in a wider context. The functions of biosphere reserves are implemented across a landscape of different uses and environmental condition.

Major functions of the UNESCO Biosphere Reserve program were traditionally described as conservation, development and logistic support (research, monitoring, education and training). These functions can now be elaborated as conservation of biodiversity, increased ecological understanding at landscape scales and, experimentation with, and demonstration of ecologically sustainable development. These are integrated through a multi-disciplined approach, focusing on 10 major objectives (after UNESCO 1995):

1. Local community participation.
2. Integrated land use management.
3. *In situ* conservation and restoration.
4. Research.
5. Monitoring.
6. Regional planning and development.
7. Environmental education and training.
8. Ecologically sustainable development.
9. Information and communication.
10. Development of an international network.

In the 1984 Action Plan these functions became generalised for practical implementation and planning as 'core', 'buffer' and 'transition' zones (UNESCO 1984, 1995, Parker 1993, Bridgewater 1994). While generally portrayed as a circular 'target' diagram, the concept refers to the need to manage land uses and functional ecological flows across an entire landscape mosaic, which also includes a socio-economic dimension. The so-called, 'core' areas are priority conservation areas (e.g., National Park or Conservation Reserve) representing regional biodiversity and, as monitoring or reference sites for adaptive management (Figure 6.1). 'Buffer' zones are really one end of a continuous transition region, extending further into an area of co-operation, where biodiversity threatening influences on the core and the surrounding landscape are minimised (Batisse 1982, 1993, Brunckhorst and Bridgewater 1994, 1995). The Multiple Use Module (MUM) described in various forms by Harris and Noss (see Noss and Harris 1986, Noss and Cooperrider 1994) is a useful extension of the Biosphere Reserve buffer zone concept where planning and management for maximum buffering capacity (minimal or no use affecting an impact on the core) occurs closest to the core; buffer zones further from the core include increased intensity of use. Figure 6.1 portrays the conceptual biosphere reserve and a more likely example of its real application.

Core areas should provide reference sites for research and monitoring in addition to monitoring of the effects of human activities across buffer and transition zones. Programs such as the Long Term Ecological Research (LTER) program in the USA (Gosz 1995) could be widely implemented using core areas as reference sites and the integrated buffer-transition zones to monitor change. Information should be fed back to local citizens and into regional and international networks and used in adapting management at a variety of scales.

In addition, biosphere reserves provide for increased community ownership and responsibility of protected areas as well as private lands, environmental restoration, monitoring and experimental ESD projects with public and private partners. A fourth zone or part of the buffer area might therefore be termed a Zone of Cooperation. The Zone of Cooperation may occur within or as part of the transition zone (as illustrated in the example of Figure 6.1), or extend well beyond the transition zone — perhaps as a network with local communities and towns. In the case of the Bookmark Biosphere bioregional project, described in this chapter, seven towns within the broader region are involved in the project. It includes coordinated management of public land through a community trust. In addition, several private landholders have requested affiliation with the project or 'donated' their land (without loss of their private title) as buffer/transition zone components of the nominated UNESCO Biosphere Reserve. This spirit of cooperation has developed voluntarily with the new partnerships and responsibility for integrated management of the bioregion, jointly acknowledging shared values and goals for an alternative, more sustainable, future. Fitzgerald River Biosphere Reserve in the south-west of Western Australia, having one of the highest diversity of endemic flora on the globe, is another interesting example. It encompasses a 'super-core' area to which no access is allowed except for scientific monitoring under strict quarantine procedures to restrict the spread of the *Phytophora* fungus which causes die-back (Watson 1993). National Park (the 'core' zone) surrounds the super-core, and this is buffered by state forest reserve. There is a transitional zone beyond this through a variegated landscape of forest remnants, riparian areas and farms. This melds with the towns and community-group activities (e.g., Landcare, Rivercare) that are the centres from which cooperative management activities emanate — a zone of cooperation.

Biosphere reserves have been compatible with (and even an operational framework for) the philosophy of sustainable development, well before this concept was promoted through the Brundtland Report (WCED 1987) and more recently through Australia's ESD Strategy (1992).

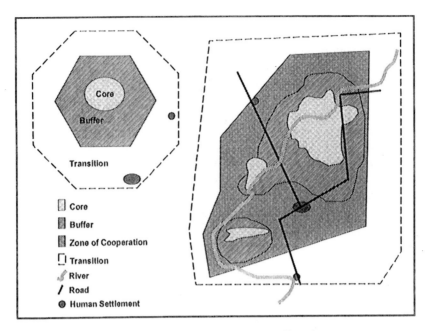

Figure 6.1. Conceptual (Left) and real application (Right) of biosphere reserve zoning.

People are an essential part of the fabric of landscapes. In recognising that there is probably no ecosystem that remains unaffected in some way by human activity, people and their activities are considered a part of a biosphere reserve (ie, beyond the 'core' protected area). They are encouraged in their participation and ownership of the program at a local level. This can be done by integrating public, private and community sectors through genuine partnerships, developing an understanding of landscape and social processes beyond ones' own patch, and being given real responsibility and an opportunity to be involved in regional landscape management. This not only encourages greater acceptance and understanding of the need to conserve biodiversity but also ensures the operation of the biosphere reserve becomes a vehicle for social and institutional transformation of attitudes, values and practices towards common goals for a sustainable future.

The concepts and principles of the MAB program were well ahead of their time. Implementation was hampered by the abject position of UNESCO internationally in the early 1980s, and by greater attention and understanding being given to more charismatic programs such as World Heritage. In retrospect, it would seem that such a complex and innovative idea at a time prior to the Brundtland report (WCED 1987) and before preparations for the UNCED 'Rio' Conference was difficult to enunciate and very hard to 'sell' to science, land (and sea) resource managers and policy sectors.

A further hurdle for the program was created in its first decade. Most countries with federal systems of government and many other nations, simply nominated to UNESCO some already protected national parks as biosphere reserves. Accordingly Canada, Australia and the USA originally nominated areas for their high conservation value and for research opportunities. Consequently, most of these have been operational at only one of the functional levels of a biosphere reserve, that corresponding to a 'core' area (i.e., a national park or conservation reserve can only be a core area, although there may be a network of core areas throughout a biosphere reserve). Until recently, all were public lands alone, from which most local people felt excluded, in terms of a sense of ownership and responsibility for its well being. The broad organisational framework required for practical implementation has also been lacking.

These elements have exacerbated mis-conceptions and hampered implementation. On one hand, extreme preservationist groups have claimed that biosphere reserve status reduced protection to a national park making it 'multiple-use'. Conversely, some industry sectors were concerned that access over large areas would be restricted. Neither are true.

In contrast, a valuable if not crucial attribute of the biosphere reserve concept is its flexibility and adaptability to a variety of situations. A further advantage of the program is the lack of rigid regulations, it has no legally binding status (it is not even tied to a convention) and is no threat to land holders, rural communities or public, private or industry sectors, contrary to claims put to the US Senate inquiry that 'sovereignty' might be effected. The UNESCO MAB biosphere reserve program simply encourages and supports, through a global network, those who wish to pursue common values and principles for sustainability.

The following case studies each highlight particular benefits from an adapted biosphere reserve approach to bioregional planning and management. The examples come from China, Kenya, Spain, USA, Mexico and Australia (Figure 6.2).

CHINA

One fifth of the world's population resides in China. It is also very rich biologically with over 10% of the global species of flowering plants and a similar proportion of the world species of amphibians, reptiles, birds and mammals. With obvious human pressure and few funds for strict nature conservation activities on natural resources, China has become actively involved in UNESCO MAB in an attempt to reconcile the interface between conservation and resource use. There are now some 35 national nature reserves associated with 10 biosphere reserves, which are encompassed in

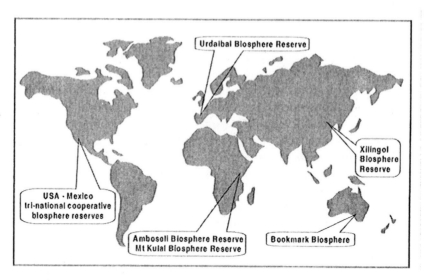

Figure 6.2. Location of case studies.

biocultural (bioregional) landscape contexts (Braatz 1992, Zhao 1995, Li *et al*. 1995).

Covering an area of almost 11, 000 sq. km, Xilingol Biosphere Reserve is the largest in China. Its elevation, averages around 1000 m (asl) and it is typical of the temperate grasslands of the Mongolian plateau. These are similar in general of the Eurasian steppes and have been grazed for thousands of years by nomadic Monguls. Used as a rangelands in this way the grasslands have been used as a sustainable natural resource. However in relatively recent times, over the past 30–50 years, degradation of the grasslands and soils has become a serious problem (Li *et al*. 1995). The main cause has been the development of, now largely sedentary, local populations and major changes on social structure, which are reflected in changed grazing regimes and increased stocking rates over smaller spatial and temporal scales (Li *et al*. 1995, Thwaites *et al*. 1995, Thwaites and Delacy 1997).

Other pressures include expanding cultivation, changes in government policy and land tenure and increasing privatisation of grazing rights and the introduction of a market economy (Li *et al*. 1995). Interestingly, these represent a move away from the principles for sustainable 'open', common property, resource access regimes described by Ostrom (1990). Privatisation may only serve to focus intensive resource use in a small area over a short time — effectively decreasing resilience and reducing scales of economy across the landscape. The privateer having mined the natural resources of that land simply sells up or abandons it to buy elsewhere. In contrast, collective action, responsibility and self-regulation build social and ecological resilience (Berkes and Folke 1998). It also serves to further illustrate the enormous importance of fully integrating and communicating the human dimension in natural resource management within the appropriate biocultural context (Saberwal and Kothari 1996).

The reduced capacity of herders to make a reasonable living from rangeland grazing has been interpreted as demonstrating the need for other kinds of diversification in the bioregion's economy (Thwaites et al. 1995, Thwaites and Delacy 1997). Community development projects include ecotourism, wildlife management and establishment of a Botanic gardens, agroforestry, and sustainable grazing through involvement of herders in demonstration projects (Li et al. 1995, Thwaites et al. 1995, Thwaites and Delacy 1997).

With the advent of bioregional (including socio-cultural) considerations through implementation of Xilingol Biosphere Reserve planning and management, areas undergoing new cultivation have been reduced. In addition, several reference areas (core areas) have been established for research and monitoring within a state run property, Baiinxile Livestock Farm, which also represents a buffer zone. The Inner Mongolia Grasslands Ecosystem Research Station of the Chinese Academy of Sciences undertakes ecological studies into the structure and function of the grassland systems and methods to increase productivity (Zhao 1995, Li et al. 1995). The research station is part of an open network of institutions, which work collaboratively in building research capacities and opportunities and sharing information.

Xilingol Biosphere Reserve is a valuable model in the management of common property resources and attempts to balance socio-cultural functions with ecological functions. It exemplifies the integration of multiple roles and functions within a bioregional context, and the development of a social and ecological monitoring, and networking capacities.

Networking and information exchange between the rangeland peoples of Xilingol and Bookmark Biosphere Reserves has resulted in recognition of an official 'Twinning' partnership arrangement.

KENYA
Mount Kulal Biosphere Reserve

The Mt Kulal Biosphere Reserve in Kenya extends across some 7,000 square kilometres encompassing the 'core' area, South Island National Park (3, 800 ha). Biophysically the region includes montane forest and arid grasslands, the latter including the Chalbi Salt Desert. Desertification is the major threat from timber use and grazing. The traditional inhabitants are four tribes of nomadic pastoralists who graze sheep, goats, cattle and camels. Conservation of remaining resources is a priority to curb further environmental and social degradation (McNeely 1988).

A program developed through the local people with the assistance of UNEP and UNESCO MAB, the Integrated Project on Arid Lands, aims to sustain local culture and the landscape ecosystems in harmony. Through very close consultation and on-going participation with local people a set of values and principles has been established and operates within the constraints of the traditional pastoral economy and culture of the tribes.

Social and ecological resilience is encouraged by collective management actions. A variety of incentives encourage citizens in the conservative use of natural resources, especially water, wildlife, fisheries, woodlands and soils, and support rehabilitation of land. Resource governance also incorporates a range of disincentives to control stocking levels and halt grazing of steep slopes. Subsequent improvement of the better grazing areas has allowed other areas to be protected or to recover. In addition, traditional 'drought reserves' were officially protected with the support of the tribes people and are only used for grazing in exceptional and long periods of drought (Lusigi 1984, McNeely 1988).

Amboseli Biosphere Reserve

Amboseli is, no doubt, one of the best-known 'big game' wildlife destinations. It is centred around Amboseli National Park, almost 400 square kilometres of semi-arid savanna, of international significance and renown. It is also centred around the main source of permanent water of a much, much larger system where the wildlife and the Maasi, with their cattle, reside. In Amboseli, the Maasi, their cattle and the wildlife converge in the dry season (Western 1994).

Like many other countries in Africa developing protected areas managed by the national government, conflict has arisen between the local people and the nationally owned wildlife and other resources (Western and Henry 1979). While Amboseli attracts around 200, 000 mostly foreign tourists each year, the income went directly into the central consolidated revenues instead of to local communities, local governments, or to the Park.

Since Amboseli National Park was declared in 1974, dialogue has slowly increased between the Kenya Wildlife Service and the local peoples on the needs of all for a sustainable future. The turning point came in 1990 when the Wildlife Service assumed authority for National Park management together with the ability to raise and retain its own revenue. By 1991 the far-sighted management of the Kenya Wildlife Service were returning almost 15% of visitor fees to local community development projects (Western 1994, Alpert 1996). A sense of ownership and responsibility for the regions natural resources was returned to the traditional inhabitants, along with the opportunity to share the benefits of income from foreign visitors. Incentives for wildlife protection, rather than competition, grew steadily as other opportunities for active community participation were implemented. These included the development of tourist concessions on Maasi ranches, craft markets and other niche tourist enterprises. In partnership with local people, the Kenya Wildlife Service, UNESCO and international training institutions, user-friendly Geographic Information Systems (GIS) modules are now becoming operational as a tool to assist the traditional pastoralists, and national park and wildlife officers in holistic resources assessment and management. Together with community infrastructure, development of wells for water supply, schools, health clinics and employment opportunities have further relieved the strain between the Maasi, wildlife and the authorities (Western 1994, Alpert 1996).

Local incentives for conservation have been employed in many other countries in Africa the sub-continent (e.g., Nepal) and South-East Asia (McNeely 1988). Of future concern is the reliance of such successes in poor or developing countries, on either overseas aid or increasingly on foreign tourism, either of which is unlikely to be long term. Further innovation is now needed to guide the development and testing of action-centred networks of learning by local communities for future sustainable living in harmony with landscape ecosystems.

These experiences, however, testify again to the efficacy of the emerging culture of 'bottom-up' and 'top-down' partnerships of equality. Integrated conservation and community development partnerships between various agencies can help synergise bioregional management concepts such as the Biosphere Reserve program through increased support and capacity building of local community-based conservation (see Western *et al.* Eds 1994).

SPAIN

Situated in northern Spain in the Basque Province of Vizcaya, the Urdaibai Biosphere Reserve encompasses 230 square kilometres of varied landscape ecosystems. These include steep mountains, gentle valleys and cultivated plains, fast flowing rivers, alluvial coastal plains and internationally significant wetlands (under the UNESCO Ramsar Convention), which flow into the Gulf of Gascony. Most of the human population live in two towns dating back to the 13th century. In recent years expanding industrial activity and urbanisation, with its accelerated pressures on the environment, have served to greatly increase local community awareness of the need for ecological sustainability, which in turn drives social sustainability (Albizuri 1995a).

Increasing community pressure on the Basque Government and a commissioned study of the region forced action. In July 1989 the government passed a unique and original legal instrument — the Law of 'Protection and Arrangement of the Urdaibai Biosphere Reserve'. The Urdaibai Law, as it has become known, states its aims explicitly as, to protect the integrity and rehabilitation of the geomorphology of the region, its flora, fauna, landscapes, waters and air (ie, its entire regional ecosystems). It states it will do this, notably from an ecologically based regional development perspective, 'by virtue of its natural, scientific, educative and cultural values for recreation and socio-economic development' (Albizuri 1995a,b).

In 1990 an over-arching authority, a Board of Management for the biosphere reserve region was established. It is based on a consultative model having representatives from all relevant agencies and chaired by the Director-Conservator, who is in charge of the biosphere reserve's management. There is also a Board of Cooperation, which is the citizen-based participative council, including representatives of interested organisations and sectoral interests (Albizuri 1995b). In 1994, following a large community participative workshop, the Board of Management developed the *Urdaibai Protocol on Sustainable Development*, which sets out the basic social and environmental values and principles guiding management and future development in the region. Following this the two Boards elaborated a *Plan of Use and Management* with specific actions to be taken on various areas, zoning for management, and a program for integrating sustainable development activities. The zoning of the region is also revolutionary in following landscape ecological flows across jurisdictional boundaries, so that 'buffer zones' incorporate riparian and other wildlife corridors or potential linkages following vegetation restoration (Albizuri 1995a,b).

The striking feature of Urdaibai Biosphere Reserve is the commitment of local people and government to such a strong, ecologically based, legal planning instrument. Even more noteworthy is the achievement, going beyond the narrow and rigid thinking of most notions of 'protection', to a vision underpinning planning and management within a broad regional context reflecting ecological and social functions; an operational bioregion.

UNITED STATES OF AMERICA AND MEXICO

The international border between the USA and Mexico cuts across a vast array of shared, landscape scale, ecological systems. Amongst these are cross-border systems important for sustaining biodiversity and the cultural diversity of Native Americans (after Ness and Ezcurra 1995):

- California Chaparral.
- Chihuahuan and Sonoran Deserts.
- Tamaulipan Thorn Scrub.
- The forests of the Californian Baja, Sierra Madre and Sky Islands.
- The wetlands of the lower Rio Grande/Rio Bravo.

The founding of biosphere reserves within or representing bioregions that overlap political jurisdictions produces unfamiliar circumstances requiring flexibility and compromise based on social contracts between different human communities, cultures, government agencies and managers, and researchers (Kaus 1993, 1995). Despite many potential impediments, several collaborative tri-national and tri-cultural (USA-Mexico-Native American), regional networks of biosphere reserves are now emerging with support and participation by the traditional native custodians of these landscapes.

One emerging model through the participation of the Tohono O'odham people involves the creation of two biosphere reserves that mirror each other. The Upper Gulf of California Biosphere Reserve (USA) and the Pinacate-Gran Desert Biosphere Reserve (Mexico) were established in 1993. In a broader regional context these contribute to a continuum with the Organ Pipe Cactus Natural Monument, Cabeza Prieta Reserve and the Tohono O'odham lands in the USA. Along the Mexican border, two new reserves, Canon de Santa Helena and Maderas del Carmen, were declared in 1994 contributing a valuable ecological corridor across the border to Big Bend National Park (Ness and Ezcurra 1995).

The international Sonoran Desert Alliance is another developing partnership of people and agencies in a self-identified bioregion straddling the USA-Mexico border. Encompassing three biosphere reserves of tri-national and tri-cultural interest, the region of the Alliance radiates for some 120 kilometres in all directions from the Organ pipe Cactus National Monument (Smith *et al.* 1995). The Alliance is working to promote collaborative protection of resources, ecologically sound economic development and better matching of public policy to local needs across multiple tiers of governments and their agencies, community and sectoral organisations. To do this it is incorporating applied research and traditional indigenous knowledge to participatory planning and management at a regional scale (Smith *et al.* 1995).

The USA, Mexico, Native American collaborative tri-national, tri-cultural alliances are another valuable example of developing bioregional models. These are remarkable for their efforts and success in overcoming considerable barriers of various kinds — international, culural, management, and the institutional cultures of several different agencies.

They are also developing a strong grass-roots (including Native American) constituency supported by more flexible arrangements of agencies and researchers.

AUSTRALIA

The UNESCO Biosphere Reserve program provides an international umbrella for developing and testing community-based adaptive-management or 'learning-by-doing' models. This approach has begun to develop at Fitzgerald River Biosphere in south Western Australia (Watson 1993) and at Bookmark Biosphere in South Australia (Brunckhorst 1996, Brunckhorst et al. 1997a).

Communities of South Australia, Victoria and New South Wales living along the Murray River are faced with a number of environmental challenges. Soil loss, landscape degradation and species loss combine with the infusion of saline ground waters, decreasing water quality, and disappearing wetlands — the liver and kidneys of the River — to collectively threaten the sustainability of all Riverland communities. The semi-arid mallee ecosystems of this region are uniquely Australian, consisting of a few *Eucalyptus* species adapted to the harsh dry conditions. Characteristically this vegetation is multi-stemmed and squamose, and possesses peculiarly shaped leaves enabling the canopy to intercept about 15% of available rainfall with a further 30% running down the multiple trunks. An extensive root system can tap water 30 metres deep and regeneration (e.g., post fire or clearing) occurs from the roots. Seed germination requires fire.

Productivity of this mallee ecosystem is low. The region receives an average of 240 millimetres of annual rainfall with annual evaporation rates potentially greater than 2,300 millimetres. Droughts are frequent and are punctuated with erratic floods. Soils are fragile and poor with deficiencies in structure and nitrogen content. The hydrology of the floodplain and wetlands of the Murray River has been altered by a variety of engineering projects designed to support agriculture and irrigation development. Problems of salinity within the ground water have been compounded by other factors including loss of deep-rooted vegetation through land clearing for timber and pastoral use throughout the past century. Many of the land degradation problems within the biosphere reserve are replicated on lands scattered throughout the drainage of the Murray River and its tributary, the Darling, which together drain one-seventh of the continent.

Bookmark Biosphere covers a region of more than 7 000 square kilometres. Biophysically, the region encompasses the interconnected river, its anabranch creeks and floodplain, and mallee-eucalypt dominated uplands. This is the environment that the local communities identify with — the 'Riverland'. Several small townships occur in the region. Bookmark Biosphere is made up of more than 25 differently tenured pieces of land, including conservation reserves, game and forestry reserves, national trust land, large (private) pastoral leases and other private land. A kind of community commons covering 2,000 square kilometres is the *Calperum* pastoral lease which was purchased with funds provided jointly by a Chicago benefactor and the federal government (after strong bipartisan recommendation by a Parliamentary Standing committee; HoRSCERA 1993). It is a community focal point to trial innovative approaches to large scale restoration and novel sustainable land uses. In joining this collective together, governments have vested the community with the ownership and responsibility for selecting goals for management of this entire regional landscape.

The flood plains of Bookmark Biosphere Reserve are recognised as internationally significant wetlands for waterfowl and migratory species (e.g., RAMSAR). The 'Calperum' Pastoral Lease, which incorporates many of these wetlands of international significance, is also the focal point for the community to experiment with novel ecologically restorative industries (Brunckhorst *et al.*1997). However, large-scale landscape recovery and species restorations are necessary and integral to the pursuit of ecologically sustainable development initiatives.

The Riverland communities, through nominated representatives, manage the land within the Biosphere Reserve and accomplish required tasks through a citizens committee, the Bookmark Biosphere Trust. The community-based Trust is constituted under South Australian legislation. The Trust is the formal management body responsible for Bookmark Biosphere Reserve. State and Federal agencies and private sector professionals serve the Trust in understanding and implementing management options.

The Bookmark Biosphere Trust is an innovative and far sighted group of citizens concerned with the long term sustainability of the natural environment, social values and standard of living in the Murray Riverland of South Australia. This is indeed a bold commitment to support a 'bottom-up' culture of capacity to accomplish conservation goals with few resources, political harmony, and new productive and innovative working relationships to leverage available resources, commitment and talent. This synergy, therefore, provides for a combination resource and capacity building from 'bottom-up' (community), 'top-down (government), and sideways-in (private sector) across an experimental model bioregion.

CHAPTER 7

COASTAL AND MARINE
BIOREGIONS

Coastal zones are particularly worthy of attention because they
are the most productive, richest in species, most affected by
global change of all marine or marine-related systems. (G.
Carleton Ray et al. 1992) ... Also important is the evolution of
inter-institutional cooperation for coastal zone conservation

(G. Carleton Ray, 1991)

There is good reason to be particularly concerned about our burgeoning coastal and inshore marine problems: this is where most of us live and from which we receive our sustenance.

Throughout the world, more than 50 per cent of the population lives within one kilometre of the coast — it is expected that this population will grow by 1.5 per cent per year in the coming decade (Tolba and El-Kholy 1992). Biophysically speaking, about 20 per cent of the world's coast is sandy, backed by beach dunes, ridges and similar depositional substrate — more than 70 per cent of these have shown considerable (net) erosion over the past decade (Viles and Spencer 1995).

We still tend to think the marine environment can look after itself and often cannot see the problems and pressures across the coastal-marine interface. Marine policy makers and managers have tended to argue that because the marine environment is different it must be considered and managed separately from the adjacent land (and this seems to be strongly defended despite clear evidence to the contrary, creating further institutional impediments). The greater uncertainty of how marine systems operate has tended to encourage this tyranny of isolated management and fragmented decision-making (Odum 1982). Scientific involvement in management or policy making tends to be episodic cases of reactive crisis management. Coastal management tends to be extremely fragmented between a multitude of organisations and laws, many at odds with each other. Yet globally, there is undoubtedly enormous pressure and degradation on coastal-marine environments and resources — far greater than on any other ecological system.

Across the USA, Australia and the nations of South-East Asia, human population is growing fastest along the coastline than anywhere else. The major impacts arising from increasing population densities along the coast include:

- Loss of habitat, species and ecological services.
- Invasions by exotic species.
- Interception of water and sediment transport.
- Increasing rate of sea level rise.
- Increased pollution of inshore environments.
- Increased nutrients in coastal and inshore environments.

THE COASTAL–MARINE INTERFACE

The coastal-marine interface is perhaps the most significant ecotone on which humanity's survival depends. Land/sea systems are essentially four-dimensional, where the ocean 'atmosphere' physically supports marine life through time, and the inhabitants, species and species assemblages vary markedly in the environmental attributes on which they depend (Brunckhorst and Bridgewater 1994, 1995 a, b, Peterson and Lubchenco 1997). Oceans and inshore environments are far from homologous (Ray and Hayden 1992), however, circulation of water in the ocean and the atmosphere on land (and over water) in the coastal zone do have similarities (Peterson and Lubchenco 1997). For example, convergence is a circulation pattern common to both, though organisms (or their propogules) in the atmosphere are usually temporary residents whereas a marine convergence can be a very concentrated area of biological activity (Steele 1991). While some species and species assemblages may require relatively discrete areas amenable to protection through reservation, others utilise a range of space and resources through time and therefore require larger scale or land/seascape linkages to maintain viable populations (Steele 1991, Palmer et al. 1996). Some marine managers (e.g., Kenchington and Kelleher 1995, Ottesen and Kenchington 1995) incorrectly argue the latter signifies a major difference between land and sea systems, and that terrestrial and marine systems should be managed separately. Such linkages are as true for terrestrial systems as they are for marine, and they certainly occur across the coastal-marine interface (e.g., the fisheries of most countries are inshore and reliant on terrestrial coastal processes to sustain them; Talbot 1994). Clearly, there is a tremendous need for holistic, integrated management across the coastal marine interface. And again, it is worth repeating, the critical importance of breaking away from institutionalised concepts of natural resource management that have more to do with 'protecting' an organisations' jurisdiction than the reality of ecological or social systems.

Increasingly, therefore, scientists and managers are advocating the coastal zone be described and managed in the following context (Dyer and Holland 1991, Ray and Hayden 1992, Price and Humphries 1993, Dutton et al. 1994, Brunckhorst and Bridgewater 1994, 1995):

> The coastal-marine interface or coastal zone extends from the coastal faces of mountain ranges, their watersheds through to the waters of the continental shelf.

We must consider our seas and coasts as a terrestrial-marine interface zone, not stopping at high water mark, but as the dynamic interactions between atmosphere, land, sea, biota and human activity (Ray and Hayden 1992, Talbot 1994, Dutton and Saenger 1994, Viles and Spencer 1995, Smythe 1995). Across this coastal interface, major movements of sediments and nutrients are powered by waves, tides, currents (in water and air). These movements shape the coastal profile, contributing erosional and depositional landforms. The terrestrial component is not placid, as rivers bring sediments, nutrients and freshwater to the coast and inshore waters (Viles and Spencer 1995). As well as providing the base for extensive human settlement, the coast is home to some of the worlds most productive and diverse ecosystems (e.g., mangroves, coral reefs, saltmarshes). From a biodiversity angle, the coastal zone is mega-diverse, with beaches being the only ecosystem on earth containing representatives from every phyla (see Ray 1991, Wilson 1992). The members of coastal biodiversity are also active in forming reefs, accretions, and aiding sedimentation in addition to providing important buffering and filtering capacities (Peterson and Lubchenco 1997). All these elements are in fragile balance, controlled by physical and biological processes that can easily be upset by perturbations of natural or human origins (Figure 7.1).

From a social and cultural perspective, indigenous peoples and the citizens of the high-density communities now living on the coast generally identify with the environment across the coastal-marine interface as defined above (Castaneda 1993, Smyth 1995, Wells and White 1995).

They identify with the lower end of the catchments running into estuaries (often where townships are located and where ocean access by boat is possible), with the coastal plains for agriculture and other uses, with the beach and sea for recreation and gathering of marine resources (Ellsworth 1995, Brunckhorst and Bridgwater 1994, 1995a,b). Figure 7.1 illustrates the interaction of some influences across the coastal-marine interface.

Traditional rights, freedoms and open-access to marine resources and the marine environment generally makes future planning for protection, control or restricted access a complex issue. Consideration of innovative solutions again, opens the door for the novel partnership models and processes for integrated, regional scale, coastal-marine management (Dyer and Holland 1991, Chua 1993, Gubbay and Welton 1995, Wells and White 1995, Crance and Draper 1996).

Solutions to human impacts on coastal-marine ecosystems therefore require examination of multiple temporal and spatial levels of organisation (Chua 1993, Price and Humphry 1993, Talbot 1994, Ray and McCormick-

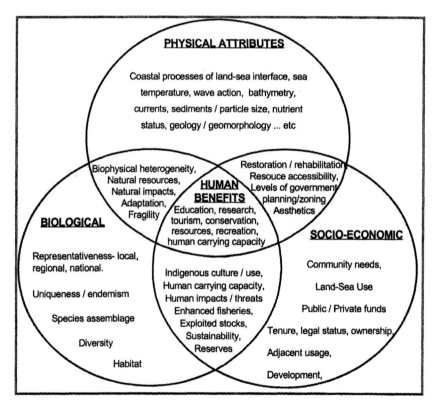

Figure 7.1. Spheres of Interaction across the Coastal-Marine Interface (after Brunckhorst and Bridgewater 1995a).

Ray 1994, Hirvonen *et al.* 1995, Viles and Spencer 1995). Resource use, development and conservation decisions should be based on assessment of both environmental and human community needs in a broad spatio-temporal context (Dyer and Holland 1991, Crance and Draper 1996).

Constraints to management of large ocean areas include:

- Limited knowledge of the human-caused interactions between lands and waters and their consequences;
- An inability to fully control events both upstream and downstream;
- The extreme difficulty of managing complex jurisdictional claims on the lands and waters included, involving national, regional, and local authorities, each highly sensitive to real or imagined encroachment;
- The difficulties involved in setting management boundaries (generally having little ecological meaning) that are clear and unmistakable for anyone to identify;
- The problems involved in assigning priority to competing resource uses or activities for these areas;
- The differences in scale of the marine systems and processes involved in these areas; and of course
- The relative lack of understanding in the public of just why it is important that these areas be established and maintained.

Even the managers of the extensive Great Barrier Reef Marine Park are now realising management planning must recognise and consider the major influences coming from the land into the more highly connected reef waters (Dutton and Saenger 1994, Talbot 1994). The reef cannot be managed separately from coastal lands, streams, wetlands and mangroves. The system of zoning apparently protects (ie, in 'core' reserved areas of IUCN Category I or II) less than 1% of the entire Great Barrier Reef in many, mostly small 'preservation zones' (Ray and McCormick-Ray 1994, Dutton *et al.* 1994, Talbot 1994, Brunckhorst and Bridgewater 1995, Brunckhorst *et al.* 1998). This is an inadequate representation of reef communities in highly protected areas and its design, in terms of position of these areas rarely reflects ecological flows or buffering of threatening processes.

Application of integrated planning and management through bioregional frameworks has real potential to deal with the issues outlined at the beginning of this chapter, but they must be implemented across the common ecologically and socially functional areas that extend across the coastal-marine interface (Chapter 9). A bioregional approach can also help break down the highly defended institutional cultures that inhibit integrated regional scale ecosystem management. This is critical if we are to deal effectively with the scale of management of human activities as well as ecological systems that effect the entire coastal zone. For example, the Great Barrier Reef might be more effectively managed through a framework other than a 3000 kilometre long, off-shore strip. Several, adjacent bioregional frameworks extending across the terrestrial coastal interface with reef waters to the continental shelf edge could be nested within a broader scale (sub-continental ecoregion) for planning more strategic management. Management of coastal watersheds (and sub-catchments) could in turn be nested within each bioregion (Chapter 9).

Therefore coastal bioregional frameworks could be considered that combine adjacent marine and terrestrial ecoregions/bioregions into a more appropriate management context. Hence coastal bioregions straddle the land-sea ecotone, which has a multitude of common driving forces and influences (Figure 7.2). Within the cultural landscape-seascape of the bioregion, these influences will include:

- the coastal uplands and streams, maintaining freshwater production (and other ecological services) and flows to the sea;
- the coastal plains with rivers, estuaries, salt marshes, mangroves, and tidal lands;
- the beach and shore zone;
- various elements of the inshore (depositional zone) and continental shelf, benthic features, reefs, islands, coastal barriers, and dynamic zones such as upwelling areas;
- towns, human settlements, recreation uses, effluent and nutrient management;
- farming and agriculture on the plains;
- management of forestry activities in lower catchments;
- access and use of fisheries and other resources.

The requirements for human settlements, agricultural production on the coastal plains, recreation along beaches and use of the estuary must be balanced with natural resource governance to sustain the ecological processes and services that land and sea jointly provide (Figure 7.2). These include, for example, the recruitment and replenishment of biophysical elements such as mangroves and fisheries, freshwater production and nutrient assimilation. Socially cooperative choices for long-term resource use and protection within a cultural land-seascape context (bioregion) can provide real benefits for value driven, partnership approaches to large scale sustainability issues across the coastal zone (Crance and Draper 1996).

Identification and selection of highly protected 'core' areas (IUCN protected area category I/II) for conserving ecological systems and processes requires a system of networking across the coastal-marine interface at multiple scales. Design and planning for comprehensive representation of bio-diversity can be accomplished by a variety of methodologies (Chapter 8). With some adaptation, these methods appear to be suited to application across the coastal-marine realm. However, they need to incorporate representation across broad scales of ecological processes, because some coastal ecosystems are low in species diversity but extremely important for their physical habitat role or ecological processes/function role (e.g., sea-grass beds, estuaries which tend to be low in species numbers but very important for their high primary productivity and filtering capacities). A 'proportional representation' approach combined with the methods suggested above would appear to be the best approach. In essence, biodiversity, species communities/habitats (or surrogates thereof) should be represented (in replicates) and protected in 'core' highly protected areas in the proportion in which they occur in the region (HoRSCERA 1993, Brunckhorst 1994, 1995, 1998, Brunckhorst and Bridgewater 1995a,b, UNESCO 1995, Steinitz et al. 1996). While rare or vulnerable species and/or processes may still require additional protection, this approach incorporates precautionary protection across areas of which little is now known. For example, supposed interstitial areas between islands, may, actually include sponge beds, soft coral assemblages, particular benthic algal communities or other habitats — especially those of the 'unseen' invertebrates. Actual areas of systems/habitats protected will still vary according to the proportion of the marine reserve that they are believed to currently cover. If a proportional approach has been taken it is more likely some 'unknown' attributes will have been protected. When a greater understanding of the distribution of species assemblages and system function is gained, adjustment for adaptive management will be easier to achieve. Adaptive design and planning for protection and buffering of important ecosystem flows and linkages will also be guided by watershed inputs, estuarine systems productivity and longshore and ocean currents.

The hypothetical example given in Figure 7.2 is very simplified and generalised. Yet it demonstrates that with relatively minor innovation in planning, it is possible to formulate and implement policies and practices with local people within an ecologically and socially meaningful regional framework. The main advance required to do this is, again, in reshaping our institutional cultures towards the partnership models described earlier in order to break down compartmental impediments and operationalise planning across jurisdictional boundaries.

Identification and selection of core areas for conserving ecological systems and processes will require planning for connectivity across the coastal-marine interface. In this case bioregions will encompass significant ecotones for ecological function as well as social function (Chapter 4).

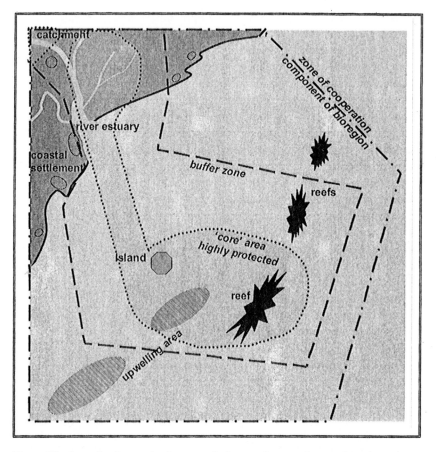

Figure 7.2. Generalised example of integrated planning framework, using biosphere reserve principles, within a bioregional context straddling the important process-driven coastal-marine interface.

Linkages might be identified along gradients that reflect system properties, such as, salinity or turbidity (Ray and Gregg 1991, Dyer and Holland 1991, Ray and McCormick-Ray 1994, Brunckhorst and Bridgewater 1994, 1995a, b). Within the bioregional framework, monitoring can focus on individual characteristics of the land-sea linkages that are measurable, comparable and scale-related functional attributes (Ray and McCormick-Ray 1994). Ecosystem management, adjustable through monitoring feedback becomes the guiding discipline for sustainable natural resource use across land and sea.

Bioregional frameworks can be an exceedingly valuable planning and management tool to deal with perilous coastal zone issues. The planning and implementation of a model similar to that of Figure 7.2 is taking shape along part of the northern New South Wales coastal zone of the central-east coast of Australia. The Coffs Harbour region includes several coastal towns, tourist resorts and fishing villages, a variety of land uses, and several rivers with an assortment of estuaries and wetlands and the Solitary Islands Marine Park. The coastal plains sections of catchments, coastal terrestrial national parks, fisheries, and local government land use planning and management are beginning to be developed in a more integrated cooperative framework.

Bioregions provide a multi-dimensional framework for managing human interactions across terrestrial and marine systems, which have their own complex and extensive inter-relationships. It is well suited to the coordinated coupling of environmental and resource management across the coastal marine realm — possibly, the ecotone of greatest consequence for sustaining nature and society.

PART IV:
BIOREGIONAL PLANNING AND MANAGEMENT

CHAPTER 8

BIOREGIONAL NETWORKS OF PROTECTED AREAS

The partnerships that are formed today ... demonstrate that protected areas — in their many forms — can contribute to guiding people in their choice by providing many goods and services of long-term benefit to a human society.

Jeffery McNeely 1995

This book is concerned with integrated natural resource management — most of which occurs outside formal conservation reserves. However, establishing bioregional networks of protected areas that represent or sample landscape ecosystems is a fundamental task in building a sustainable future. Reserves must also contribute to restoration or replenishment, buffering of potentially degrading effects and various ecological services (Daily 1997) beyond their boundaries to assist sustainable natural resource use of society. Protected natural areas are also important reference sites for monitoring and feedback of management actions and the effects of land uses elsewhere in the bioregion. Little has been written on the operational planning of land uses, including reserves, to integrate on- and off- reserve conservation with production through an ecoregional or bioregional framework for protected areas. This chapter describes strategic principles for a systems approach to the development of regional reserve networks. Policy makers and planning professionals will find this adequate for their purposes. For those interested in the details of particular methodologies, a list of authorities is given at the end of the chapter.

Existing systems of protected areas, terrestrial or marine, do not adequately represent the diversity of ecosystems and species assemblages. Until relatively recently reserve selection was not directed towards preserving biodiversity. Areas selected as national parks and similar reserves tended to be chosen for their spectacular scenery, value for recreation, special features or, because they consisted of very steep terrain which could not be developed for some other land use.

Often, reserves have been chosen purely on the basis of *ad hoc* political decisions (Pressey 1994). It is also likely that many existing reserves are unsustainable for protecting biodiversity in the longer term, because of size, shape, landscape connectivity of ecological systems, landscape and climate change, and inconsistent application of management principles (Hudson 1991). For example, the existence of habitat corridors and the matrix of other natural or semi-natural areas, threatening processes from the surrounding landscape (use of pesticides, vegetation clearing, soil loss), patch dynamics and the required range of larger animals and birds will effect long-term resilience of protected areas. The need to make land use decisions on a bioregional basis, therefore, is not only desirable to the process of ecologically sustainable development, but is necessary for protecting biodiversity based on ecological rationale.

Some mining companies, and other industry sectors, quite rightly criticise governments for a preoccupation with 'real estate' (i.e., percentage area of the country protected) rather than ecology in identifying protected areas. It is no longer realistic to merely look at the percentage area of a nation or region that is protected for conservation purposes, nor can the significance of a reserve be determined by size alone. For example, a large area reserved in the wrong place may contribute little to conservation goals, but may restrict future options for reserves where they are really needed to protect ecological processes and habitats that are not represented elsewhere in the reserve system (Pressey *et al.* 1993). In practice, the custodians of protected areas (i.e., human society represented by local communities) generally require compromise because of competing land uses and traditional values (Ishwaran 1992, Nelson and Serafin 1992, Western 1994). In the light of the deficiencies of *ad hoc* proclamation of reserves that may not be ecologically viable let alone contribute broader scale elements for sustainability (e.g., habitat connectivity, water cleansing, carbon sinks), more robust and defensible methods for selection of new reserves have been evolving rapidly (e.g., Margules *et al.* 1988, 1994, Rebelo and Siegfried 1992, Scott *et al.* 1991, 1993, Saetersdal 1993, Pressey *et al.* 1993, Risser 1995, Woinarski *et al.* 1996, Church *et al.* 1996).

A BIOREGIONAL APPROACH TO RESERVE SELECTION

From the above discussion it is clear that one critical element of any integrated plan to sustain biodiversity and ecological processes will be a system of conservation reserves (strictly or legally protected areas), which should be explicitly designed and managed to represent and protect the diversity of gene pools, species and ecosystems across many scales of interaction. In order to meet these goals we need to identify and plan regional reserve networks that:

- sample all biogeographic regions (ecoregions/bioregions);
- sample most biological diversity within a region;
- provide connectivity across a landscape; i.e., between patches and along ecotones (which may shift with climate change);
- are large enough to contain particular landscape scale ecological processes that need to be protected as part of bioregional reserve networks (e.g., wetlands and interconnecting streams for nutrient uptake and water cleansing);
- contain multiple representations of each species and system to guard against catastrophic events; and
- incorporate viable areas and numbers of each species and ecosystems to provide optimal chances for long term retention of biological diversity.

The first step in establishing an ecologically representative protected area system is to achieve agreement about how to interpret the environment in a way that indicates what should be represented. The advantage of using a flexible, hierarchical environmental regionalisation to assist delineation of ecoregions and bioregions is in the potential they provide for a nationally and internationally agreed basis for identifying priority areas for increasing the representation of ecological diversity in 'core' reserves (Belbin 1993, Margules *et al.* 1994, Brunckhorst and Bridgewater 1994, 1995, Thackway and Cresswell 1995, Brunckhorst *et al.* 1998). The nested hierarchy of regions also provides a global-to-local framework for assessment and monitoring of protected areas within, and across, the regional frameworks (e.g., ecodomains, ecoregions, bioregions, landscapes, patches; see Chapter 2).

From a hierarchy of ecoregions to bioregions and ecological systems, it is possible to gain a basic impression of the bioregions where protected areas may need to be established, upgraded, expanded or linked. By comparing the proportional area of each bioregion currently represented in protected areas and the bias in the representation of ecosystems within that system of reserves, an assessment of comprehensiveness (Box 8.1) of biodiversity protection through reservation can be attained (Thackway and Cresswell 1995, Brunckhorst *et al.* 1998).

The planning framework provided by cultural bioregions — those communities people identify with — are instruments by which conservation, ecologically sustainable development and local community objectives might be integrated. Delineation of potential new protected areas will use known species distributions or incorporate biophysical and ecological criteria as surrogates of detailed biological survey data where these are not available (see Chapter 3). Such data are also useful in modelling or predicting species distributions in geographic information systems (Busby 1991, Belbin 1993). To further advance these techniques there is a need for transparency of data records, including national standards for collecting point based (i.e., scale independent) environmental and biological data, and nationally consistent standards for the free flow of data between institutions and all levels of government (Thackway and Cresswell 1993).

Operational definitions that give rise to explicit goals and measures of success in the development of an adequate, comprehensive and representative reserve system are given in Box 8.1.

There is no doubt that in order to protect and maintain more viable areas as well as populations of species and their interactions, larger reserves while minimising perimeter length, are better than smaller ones (the SLOSS debate; see Soulé and Simberloff 1986, Soulé 1991, Grumbine ed. 1994, Noss and Cooperrider 1994). Realistically however, it is much more likely that future size and shape choices of potential reserves will be severely limited. Nonetheless, larger protected areas are generally considered best, with the preference to maximise the area to perimeter ratio to minimise 'edge effects' (Soule and Simberloff 1986, Rebelo and Siegfried 1992). Multiple samples or replicates should, ideally be included in an adequate reserve system. Any measure of success will depend on many factors including management of threatening processes, size of a taxon or species assemblage and its population dynamics and energy needs, as well as environmental attributes and variables. In short, the landscape mosaic is complex ecologically and sociologically, and will differ in extent between and among bioregions, hence a range of measures will be required. The choice of potential sites based on their role in representing regional biodiversity and landscape connectivity is crucial to wise decision making. Practical management to sustain biodiversity and ecological function for production of natural resources will necessarily occur at the landscape scale because that is the scale of human activity (Western et al. 1994, Walton and Bridgewater 1996, Berkes and Folke 1998). The challenge, therefore, is to develop regional landscape management plans incorporating protected areas as some of a variety of land uses adaptively managed in the much broader, bioregional context.

A key component of any such plans is the regional reserve network. In

---

Box 8.1 Definition of Terms for Development of Protected Area Systems

System - refers to a group of objects or sites related or interacting on the basis of known or specified criteria so as to form a collective unity. Parts of a system must relate or complement each other in some way. For example, regional reserve networks may collectively form a nationwide system by representing diversity within and across a bioregional planning framework.

Adequacy - refers to the capacity of a protected area system to maintain biological diversity and ecological processes. (Adequacy will depend on the regional setting and variety of processes involved, but may include, for example: temporal and spatial perturbations, both natural and human induced; population viability; size and design of individual reserves; redundancy; and, the ability to maintain ecosystem services at a quality that meets present and future needs of native species and local human communities)

Comprehensiveness - refers to the degree to which the protected area system encompasses the entire variety of biological species and communities, ecological attributes, and physical features on a nationwide basis, as evaluated against national criteria.

Representativeness - refers to the extent that sites identified for, or already declared as, protected areas sample known biological diversity, environmental and ecological patterns and processes, and physical features at various scales Any measure of representativeness will be a function of scale.

(after Brunckhorst in HoRSCERA 1993, Brunckhorst 1994)

---

application, because of a variety of cultural and social determinants, the most likely outcome will be a mix of sizes and shapes of variously protected natural areas across a matrix of semi-natural and altered landscapes. Planners must also consider strategies for potential new protected areas that contribute restoration and landscape connectivity of ecological processes (or enlargement of existing reserves) to ensure viability and comprehensive representation, within and across bioregions. Protected areas must not simply represent biological diversity to the fullest possible extent; they must protect ecological linkages and functional processes of whole regions.

Identifying and Selecting Protected Area Networks Within Bioregions

Explicit reserve identification and selection methods have the potential to minimise the development uncertainty concerns of industry, reducing investment risk and consequently contribute important elements to a bioregional planning framework for conservation and sustainable development initiatives (Brunckhorst 1994, 1995). They are also scientifically and politically defensible in assigning a defined conservation value.

The distinction is made here between the identification process and the selection process in developing reserve systems. *Identification* relates to the procedure, whereby known biological and environmental attributes of a region (c.f. anthropogenic criteria such as 'naturalness'; see Taylor 1990) are analysed to identify all potential sites for reservation (the most comprehensive and representative of the desired features). Actual *selection* of reserves or a reserve network will often depend on a number of competing factors especially those relating to the aspirations of the local communities and social and economic issues (see Soulé 1986, Grumbine ed. 1994). Selection of the final reserve network is therefore the next step in which scientific principles and, environmental and social objectives can be maintained or maximised through flexibility in choosing the best solution while maintaining an explicit representation target (Margules *et al.* 1988, Pressey *et al.* 1993, 1994).

Step by step (iterative) procedures assist the scientific decision making process so that defensible conservation values of each site are elucidated and all possible options and combinations of reserves for a region can be considered (e.g., Kirkpatrick 1983, Margules *et al.* 1988, Pressey and Nicholls 1989, Nicholls and Margules 1993). Ignoring the identification process and selecting reserves based on opportunistic, *ad hoc*, or political decisions alone are unlikely to contribute to the protection of biological diversity, but are likely to severely limit future options for reservation.

Reserve networks cannot effectively help to conserve biodiversity unless there is an adequate ecological database and an accepted procedure for using it to identify the location of potential reserves. Spatial and geographic information systems are becoming recognised as useful tools in this process, in addition to assisting in modelling surrogate information sets (as an interim measure) where comprehensive biological survey data are lacking or unlikely to be obtained (Belbin 1993, Margules *et al.* 1994).

But critical, wise decisions are required now (Lovejoy 1995). Collation and use of available data should be an immediate priority, because land use decisions will continue to be made regardless of database adequacy. Reducing uncertainty for both conservation and sustainable development purposes is therefore critical. While there is an ongoing requirement for more data on which decisions can be based, through biological surveys and techniques for rapid biodiversity assessment, decisions about the location and management of reserves and the use of natural resources often have to be made without knowledge of the full implications (Margules and Nicholls 1984, Reid and Miller 1989, Margules and Austin 1991, Pressey et al. 1994). New reserves must be carefully selected so that limited resources are used effectively and decisions are strong and defensible. Additional data, as it becomes available, can be incorporated into decision making through adaptive management. A bioregional context for land use assessment provides a flexible landscape context in which this can successfully occur (Brunckhorst et al. 1998).

Several useful techniques for the identification of priorities for reservation have been developed based on phylogenetic or taxonomic priority (Vane-Wright et al. 1991, Woinarski et al. 1996), floristic diversity, (Rebelo and Siegfried 1992, Saetersdal et al. 1993), and gap analysis (Scott et al. 1991, 1993, Strittholt and Boerner 1995, Kiester et al. 1996). Advances have also been made in the development of a number of reserve selection procedures known as iterative methods (Kirkpatrick 1983, Margules et al. 1988, Pressey and Nicholls 1989, Bedward et al. 1992). These methods use various algorithms, which may start from different points, such as from the species richest site or where there are unique occurrences (centres of endemism), and then they generally add sites with the most new species.

Three fundamental principles for selecting priority sites and regional reserve networks have been elucidated by Bob Pressey and colleagues (Pressey et al. 1993). The principles are concerned with the ways in which individual sites/reserves relate as landscape elements of a bioregional network of protected areas. The first, *complementarity*, refers to the contribution each new area makes to existing areas or previous choices in terms of representing features not included elsewhere and it can provide a measure of comprehensiveness. The second principle, *flexibility*, acknowledges that within a given spatial context such as a bioregion, different combinations of sites may be available to form a representative protected area network. The more networks that can be assessed, the more likely the planner is to find one that is representative and maximises values of design and land suitability, and/or minimises financial cost and competition with other land uses. The third principle, *irreplaceability*, provides a fundamental way of measuring the conservation value of any site. An irreplaceable site will appear in every analysis of alternative combinations of sites; significant options for representative protection are lost if the site is excluded (Pressey *et al.* 1993, 1994a,b, Pressey 1994).

The three principles can be applied at different scales. At a national scale, they can help identify priority regions for conservation efforts; within regions or at a local level they can be used to develop representative networks of reserves. Set in a bioregional planning framework, reserve networks can be seen and valued for their contribution to sustaining landscape processes and also as contributing to sustainable land (or sea) resource use (Stritholt and Boerner 1995, Brunckhorst and Bridgewater 1994, 1995, Brunckhorst *et al.* 1998).

Experience in Australia also suggests another 'efficiency' factor in the strategy of protection by reservation. Economic costs of reserve establishment and initial management infrastructure and ecological 'efficiency' or effectiveness appears to start reducing considerably when the proportion of regional ecosystems (not area) represented in the reserve network reaches about 70–75% (within a bioregion). At this point, off-reserve measures become more efficient in contributing conservation benefits and landscape connectivity (Brunckhorst in HoRSCERA 1993, Sattler pers. comm. 1993, Pressey pers. comm. 1993, Brunckhorst *et al.* 1998).

Clearly, no protected area network can, by itself, sustain ecological processes. The role of protected area networks is to assist maintenance of ecological processes and biodiversity. Unless national, regional and local systems of reserves are chosen efficiently, it is likely that they will not sample biological diversity adequately prior to the options to do so being exhausted. Therefore, the most efficient bioregional protected area networks will sample more biological diversity in fewer sites; but again, this requires excellent management of those reserves and other landscape elements in the bioregional context to ensure sustainability of all elements. It is the landscape context that is crucial. Landscape linkages must be addressed within the holistic bioregional planning framework for sustainable land and resource use if biodiversity and ecological processes are to be sustained (Grumbine 1994, Kim and Weaver 1994).

Standards for Consistent Management

How do we tell exactly what is protected and how well that protective classification is applied and managed so that regional reserve networks are ecologically sustainable? The classification of protected areas requires rationalisation and clarification in many countries. In Australia, for example, there are almost 60 different types of protected areas across three jurisdictions of government (Federal, State and Local), and these have been declared under more than 30 pieces of legislation and a variety of planning instruments of local authorities.

Other federated nations such as Germany, Canada and the USA have similar inconsistencies of protected area management objectives between jurisdictions. Such differences in nomenclature and inconsistencies in the level of protection provided for any particular site make it difficult to gain a clear perspective of the adequacy of existing reserves to meet conservation goals. This greatly impedes progress in strategic planning and active adaptive management. In order to understand exactly what is protected and the clear intent of the management for each protected area, it is important that all of the different protected area types be assessed against an agreed system of classification such as that provided by the IUCN (1994).

In the international realm, the International Union for the Conservation of Nature (IUCN) plays a role in coordinating standards of management, principles, practices and other recommendations for the declaration and management of conservation reserves of all kinds, collectively referred to as 'protected areas'. The IUCN (1994) defines a protected area as:

> *An area of land and/or sea especially dedicated to the protection and maintenance of biological diversity, and of natural and associated cultural resources, and managed through legal or other effective means. (IUCN 1994)*

Nine major purposes of protected areas were identified by the IUCN (1994). These give rise to an identified primary objective or intent of management. In consultation with its member states, the IUCN then developed a set of six categories of protected area based on the primary purpose for which they are managed (Box 8.2).

Category I   Highly protected Area for: Ia, Scientific; or Ib, Wilderness (e.g., Nature Reserve)

Category II   Ecosystem conservation and recreation (e.g., National Park)

Category III Conservation of specific natural feature/s (e.g., Natural Monument)

Category IV   Conservation through active management intervention (e.g., Managed Species or Habitat Area)

Category V   Extensive protected area managed for Landscape/Seascape conservation and recreation (e.g., protected Landscape)

Category VI   Protected area for sustainable use of natural ecosystems (e.g., Managed Resource protected Area)

A highly protected, restricted access reserve such as a category I protected area has no appreciable resource use and minimal management input. National parks or Natural Monument reserves (category II and III type protected areas) have increasing levels of use and management, while categories IV, V and VI have a much higher intensity of management and direct resource use (Box 8.2).

This set of categories also provides for different types or groupings of protected areas to be nested within or adjacent to each other. For example, Biosphere Reserves might contain one or more category I/II (core) protected areas surrounded by a category III or IV buffer zone, which might be nested in an area (category V) of complementary conservation land uses (Bridgewater *et al.* 1996). All these specially protected and other land use areas could nest in a bioregional zone of cooperation, a category VI area, managed in an manner incorporating conservative use of resources and integrated management. Therefore, the strategic potential for the applica-

Box 8.2 IUCN protected Area Categories and their Management Objectives

(after IUCN 1994)

Management Objective *	Ia	Ib	II	III	IV	V	VI
Scientific research	1	3	2	2	2	2	3
Protect wilderness	2	1	2	3	3	-	2
Protect Biodiversity	1	2	1	1	1	2	1
Maintain ecological services	2	1	1	-	1	2	1
Protect specific natural / cultural features	-	-	2	1	3	1	3
Tourism and recreation	-	2	1	1	3	1	3
Education	-	-	2	2	2	2	3
Sustainable use of natural resources	-	3	3	-	2	2	1
Maintain cultural attributes	-	-	-	-	-	1	2

* 1 = primary objective; 2 = secondary objective; 3 = potentially applicable

tion of the categories for consistent management objectives actually lies in their multiple use within bioregions (Figure 8.1). As we have seen in the case studies, using a variety of protected area types along side or surrounding each other provides various levels of protection of biodiversity and ecological services that maintain sustainable production and human use of natural resources. In this way multiple scales of protection, management and use can be planned and implemented providing for buffering or transitional areas, areas temporarily protected for restoration and zones for community co-operation in working towards ecologically sustainable resource use (see Chapter 6, Figure 6.1). Figure 8.1 illustrates conceptually how the IUCN categories relate to each other in a bioregional management framework with the goal of sustaining both natural and social/cultural systems.

By using the IUCN management definitions and categories it will be possible to assess and monitor explicitly what is reserved (irrespective of whether managed by government, industry, trusts like The Nature Conservancy, institutions like universities or private individuals). By combining information on the (IUCN) management categories of reserves with coordinated management across multiple reserves (nested or adjacent), together with off-reserve management it is possible to start to build an

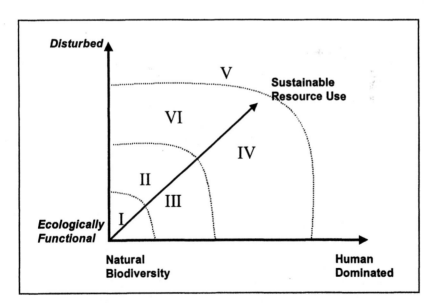

Figure 8.1. Conceptual representation of protected area category in relation to potential bioregional management functions. The value and use of nested protected areas for integrating conservation and sustainable use in a strategic bioregional planning and management framework.

operative, integrated bioregional management strategy. The nested hierarchy affords several spatial and temporal levels of integration for different kinds of reserves and sustainable use of natural resources. A bioregional management strategy will then guide strategic integration and coordination of planning and management for buffer zones, sustainable land uses, restoration and, monitoring and comparison of reference sites. Furthermore, application of IUCN categories for protected areas within strategic bioregional frameworks will provide cross-jurisdictional consistency and coordination (e.g., across State or international borders, private reserves/Trusts, and across agency jurisdictions). To further facilitate this, a common nomenclature for protected areas, which corresponds to the IUCN categories might be adopted. Novel partnerships and arrangements for improved and efficient management can then be adopted between agencies, governments and local communities as discussed in Chapter 5.

Consultation with the General Public

Involving the community in the identification, selection and management of protected areas is increasingly demanded by the public and special interest groups. In addition, governments are beginning to recognise that community involvement is vital in achieving goals for nature conservation and ecologically sustainable development without compromising the values of these areas to future generations.

Some of the advantages of public and community involvement in national parks and reserves in a bioregional context were characteristics of some of the case studies presented. These include: broader consultation which takes in a range of community needs and aspirations; access by managers to a larger reservoir of knowledge and expertise; reduction in conflict within the community; community education about conservation and sustainable resource use; fostering a sense of local ownership, responsibility and control; hands on, cost-effective assistance through 'friends of' groups, volunteers, advisory committees; and, development of an ethos which carries on to engage complementary community action outside of reserves.

Fostering public involvement in the identification, selection and management of protected areas should be an important objective of agencies, conservation groups and Trusts. Some strategies for fostering community engagement and an on-going interest in management are given in Box 8.3.

While the benefits of public involvement and ownership in planning and management of protected areas are clear, there are two main issues which governments and their agencies need to consider. First, the trade-offs between management efficiency and the increased social benefits (e.g., education) and management effectiveness gained through public involvement and support. Second, the degree to which management and planning

Box 8.3.   Strategies for fostering community engagement and an on-going interest in protected area management.

1. Clear advertising of management proposals

2. Specific public education and consultative programs

3. Inviting comment prior to proclamation of protected areas

4. Inviting public/community input prior to preparation of management plans

5. Feedback to the general public as well as contributing citizens or groups on the use of their input

6. Inviting comment on plans of management prior to their finalisation

7. Establishment of community management advisory committees

8. Shared responsibility for 'on-ground' management within and around the protected area

9. Providing for, and encouraging the establishment of, "friends of" groups or volunteer groups for each protected area

10. Funding and facilitation of complementary, community-based biodiversity and environment protection programs (outside reserves) implemented in a bioregional framework

11. Incentives which encourage community/voluntary groups and individuals to undertake complementary land management projects

12. Fostering meaningful community / public / private partnerships with shared but real responsibility of elements of management

should provide public decision-making as distinct from consideration being given to the views of the public when decisions are made by government.

For many members of the public, the scope they are given to comment on local land use proposals represents the only opportunity they have to be consulted on matters which affect conservation. Coordinated conservation areas or biosphere reserves offer a meaningful opportunity for communities to be given responsibility and to be empowered to direct their future (Watson 1993, Western et al. 1994, Brunckhorst et al. 1997).

A FINAL WORD ON PROTECTED AREAS

Protected natural areas and other reserves are a necessary element, but not complete solution for maintaining biodiversity. Even a comprehensive protected area system is not a panacea for sustaining ecological diversity — most biodiversity will always be found outside the reserve system. A network of 'core' reserves (afforded strict legal protection) is important, but only a part of a planned, balanced framework for sustaining functional ecological and production systems along with clean air and water across large regional expanses. Ultimately, an adequate conservation strategy depends on a variety of successful policies applied effectively outside reserves to ensure protection of landscape and seascape scale ecological functions, habitat restoration and ecologically sustainable resource use. Protected areas should also function as reference sites — essentially, measuring sticks for adaptively managing for landscape wide conservation and sustainable resource use objectives (e.g., Long Term Ecological Monitoring or Reference Sites; Gosz 1995, Marshall et al. 1996).

Ecosystem approaches need to be more broadly based to enhance natural resource protection and maintenance of ecological functions across entire regional landscapes, if reservation efforts are to remain viable. Therefore, networks of protected areas must also be managed in concert with all other land uses within and across a bioregion. Such a landscape approach is essential for integrating and coordinating, in a complementary way, conservation on formal reserves, conservation outside reserves, sustainable land use and community action (Saunders 1990, Strittholt and Boerner 1995, Norton and Ulanowicz 1992). Further distinction may be necessary between an individual landowner's enterprise goal of sustainable land use and the community's objective of regional biodiversity conservation through sustainable land management. Landscape elements may then be defined through integrated planning for management across jurisdictions, including; for example, protection, restoration, sustainable production and land stewardship encompassing management of feral animals, weeds, fire and water quality.

Protected areas are, or should be, of value to the custodians, local people, who share responsibility for conservation across the landscape, both within and outside protected areas. Bioregional frameworks provide a valuable context to plan, build, monitor and manage protected natural components of human dominated landscapes — in order that collectively all might contribute to the long term sustainability of each other.

READING LIST ON RESERVE SELECTION METHODOLOGIES

Readers interested in the details of specific techniques on reserve identification and selection are referred to the many published papers (e.g., Kirkpatrick 1983, Margules *et al.* 1988, Diamond 1975, Soulé and Simberloff 1986, Margules *et al.* 1988 1994, Pressey and Nicholls 1989, Scott *et al.* 1991, 1993, Rebelo and Siegfried 1992, Bedward *et al.* 1992, Saetersdal 1993, Nicholls and Margules 1993, Saetersdal *et al.* 1993, Pressey 1994, Pressey *et al.* 1993, 1994a, 1994b, Margules and Nicholls 1994, Woinarski *et al.* 1996, Church *et al.* 1996, Kiester *et al.* 1996, Brunckhorst *et al.* 1998) The Journals; *Environmental Conservation*, *Conservation Biology* and the *Natural Areas Journal* regularly publish papers on this topic. Whole books are also available on protected area conservation and reserve design issues (e.g., Soulé ed. 1986, 1987, Wilson 1992, HoRSCERA 1993, Noss and Cooperrider 1994, Grumbine ed. 1994, Forey *et al* 1994). Full citations are included in the reference list at the end of the book.

CHAPTER 9

ECOSYSTEM MANAGEMENT WITHIN AND ACROSS BIOREGIONS

Conservation is getting nowhere because it is incompatible with our Abrahamic concept of land. We abuse land because we regard it as a commodity belonging to us. When we see land as a community to which we belong, we may begin to use it with love and respect.

Aldo Leopold, 1949.

REGIONAL ECOSYSTEM MANAGEMENT

Ecosystem management has a variety of connotations for people with varying interests in natural resources. Aldo Leopold introduced the essence of ecosystem management via concepts of a land ethic, the nested hierarchy of the environment and the need to balance ecological, social and economic factors (without incapacitating ecological processes). It is, however, only in recent decades that 'ecosystem management' became a useful expression in negotiation to bring environmentalists, resource developers and land managers to round-table discussions, initially based on few common values. Interpretation of the concept vacillated considerably between those who emphasised the term 'ecosystem', for ecological sustainability, viability and integrity requirements, and those who emphasised the word 'management' from the point of view of access and use of particular environmental resources (Tuchmann *et al.* 1996). The terminology, however, has rapidly evolved through conceptual stages into a major internationally recognised discipline in recent years, and is continuing to advance through landscape ecology application development (see Grumbine ed. 1994, Forman 1995, ESA 1995, O'Neill *et al.* 1997).

A working group of the Ecological Society of America described ecosystem management as:

> ... *management driven by explicit goals, executed by policies, protocols and practices, and made adaptable by monitoring and research based on our best understanding of the ecological interactions and processes necessary to sustain ecosystem structure and function.*

ESA Ad Hoc Committee on Ecosystem Management (1995)

While this definition is very broad, it does suggest we must act on current knowledge while gathering more information, and that strategic planning is required for good management. The committee went on to emphasise eight operational principles that must be elements of ecosystem management (after ESA 1995):

1. Actions must aim to be sustainable over the long term (the intergenerational principle).
2. Strategic planning for management requires clear operational goals.
3. Incorporate the best available ecological models and understanding.
4. Develop an understanding and strategies to incorporate issues of complexity and interconnectedness of systems.
5. Consider the dynamic nature of ecological systems.
6. Incorporate and develop strategies for context and scale considerations.
7. Acknowledge the presence of humans as elements of ecological systems.
8. Be flexible and adaptable in implementation and, accountable (through monitoring).

While progress to implement these goals and principles is difficult, ecosystem management is now considered to be at the leading edge of multi-disciplinary efforts for holistic management, restoration, and sustainable use of natural resources (ESA 1995). It is generally understood to consider a broader scale than site-based research and management applications and includes management of human activities across ecosystems (and urban areas). Ecosystem management includes elements of landscape ecology which consider the spatial relationships between structural and functional components, including human elements. Landscape traits are emphasised, such as connectivity, avoidance of fragmentation, protection of catchments and identification and protection of critical habitat components. Greater understanding of patch dynamics (in four dimensions) and the multiple scales of interaction and connectivity across terrestrial, aquatic and marine systems, coupled with landscape ecology and hierarchy theory has contributed to the current expansion of interest in the potential of ecosystem management as a tool for protecting and sustaining biodiversity and natural resources (see Grumbine 1994). Changes in the mosaic of landscape ecological pattern can adversely effect biodiversity, ecological processes and services and productivity (see Forman 1995, Daily 1997). Sustaining and restoring landscape patterns that will conserve most, if not all, natural processes and functions across a region is integral to ecosystem management and a sustainable future. Nonetheless, it is becoming more and more evident that people are the key factor — spatially distributed as they are in urban areas and local regional communities (e.g., McBeth and Foster 1994, Holmes and Day 1995, Tisdell 1995, Steinitz et al. 1996).

While providing a new framework to comprehensively address complex human-environmental management issues, ecosystem management poses several challenges to traditional decision making and governance institutions. One of the most difficult aspects of devising large-scale environmental planning and management strategies is coordinating actions across public and private property boundaries. To land managers, private property owners may be seen as an obstruction to ecosystem management, or as partners to create efficient ecosystem protection. Understanding more about how programs have dealt with private property issues is critical to planning any ecosystem level management program. It is important to consider a broad spectrum of property rights, from access rights based on customary use, to rights of lessees, to the rights of traditional indigenous inhabitants.

I have argued that bioregional frameworks provide an appropriate, and pragmatic, biocultural landscape context in which to plan and implement ecosystem management across private and public land tenures. To do so we must encourage a new view of government and public agencies — one that views them as facilitators and partners with local people, rather than regulators and administrators of authority. Bioregions also provide a more meaningful framework with which to examine ecological processes and an appropriate context for implementation of adaptive management with local communities through action-centred networks and learning-by-doing. Practical application of such adaptive management requires common networks of reference sites and transects of monitoring sites across the gradation of land uses typical of the bioregion. Such reference sites provide a barometer for social flexibility and help deal with the risk and uncertainty of multi-scale interactions of society and ecology (see Walters and Holling 1990, Smil 1993, Dovers et al. 1993, Haney and Power 1996). This not only empowers local people (as well as agencies) with meaningful responsibility, it provides a mechanism to consider novel sustainable resource uses and ecologically restorative industries matched to ecological functional capacity and emergent social transformations (Hawken 1993, Brunckhorst *et al.* 1997a). Ultimately, the success of bioregional frameworks for holistic, landscape scale, ecosystem management will depend on the awareness and understanding of those who live in and live from these land/sea scapes and those involved in policy, planning and decision making.

THE MISAPPLICATION OF ECOSYSTEM MANAGEMENT TO WATERSHEDS AND CATCHMENTS

One place where the principles of ecosystem management have been applied with varying success is in the management of watersheds and catchments. Aquatic ecosystems and water catchments all over the world are under enormous pressures of threatening, degrading processes wrought by human population. Water management tends to be highly fragmented across a variety of jurisdictions and legislated mandates (Cortner and Moote 1994, Allan *et al.* 1997). Noss and Cooperrider (1994) succinctly summarise the peculiar connectivity of the hydrologic cycle and the threats to it, which include:

- point source contaminants (e.g., industry, acid-mine drainage, effluent dumping);
- non-point pollution (e.g., from agricultural run-off);
- resource access development (e.g., logging, vegetation clearance, domestic stock access, roads and drainage, dams, channel diversions, water extraction);
- loss of habitat, particularly riparian vegetation and wetlands;
- loss of natural periodic cycles of flood and drying; and,
- introduction of exotic flora and fauna.

Holistic approaches to resource management, particularly for the monitoring and management of water quality issues, have developed in various forms. Watershed and catchment management, in particular, is based on the accurate model of streams and rivers as linear, down-slope transport systems. In several countries, such as Australia and the USA, these approaches have gained considerable popularity with resource management agencies and through community-based management committees.

The adoption of natural boundaries to delineate management jurisdictions certainly demonstrates some institutional adaptation and innovation that is most welcome. However in many cases, agency programs have tended to remain compartmentalised. A fair generalisation is that most catchment management activities have been local, site-based remediation of symptoms rather than strategic planning and management of causal factors along whole watersheds.

Not withstanding the institutional impediments elaborated earlier (Chapter 4), there are several current misapplications of catchment management concepts that need to be remedied before they become institutionally entrenched. (Griffith and Omernik 1991, Griffith et al. 1994, Omernik 1995, Statzner et al. 1997, Allan et al. 1997, Omernik and Bailey 1997).

Finding an operational framework for catchment management

Catchments collect and integrate elements of the landscape systems through which they pass. Because watersheds and their streams are not found in all landscapes, they cannot provide a unifying management context for all places. This is particularly true across the ancient, flat, dry land of Australia where, for the most part, streams do not exist and surface water is ephemeral. Parts of other continents, such as North America and Africa, also exhibit extensive landscapes where the fragmentation of streams, related cycles of wet and drying, drive the system rather than linear downstream transport models (Stanley et al. 1997).

In landscapes with flowing rivers, it may be rare that local or regional communities identify with an entire watershed or have a real interest in the distant, downstream portions of the catchment. Biophysical elements, including vegetation, topography and streams, are important factors influencing patterns of human settlement and land use. Permanent streams attract urban and rural development, usually at their lower reaches, where historically they provided transportation for urban industry, and irrigation for agriculture. Managing an extensive watershed, such as the Murray-Darling in Australia, or the Columbia in North America, may force partnerships among dissimilar communities along vast linear distances, while ignoring the natural affinities of communities at comparable levels in different watersheds.

It appears that it is common for watersheds to pass through (at least) three distinct biophysical landscapes, each with different soils, vegetation, climate, precipitation elevation and mean slope; and subsequently different land uses (Omernik and Griffith 1991, Adinarayana et al. 1994, Allan et al. 1997, O'Neill et al. 1997) and socio-economic settings of local communities (Figure 9.1). It is with these landscapes (a bioregional sub-catchment) that local people identify with most strongly. The substrate, sediment, chemical and biological characteristics of the stream at any one point will reflect the attributes of the region through which it has been passing. While considering the bigger context of the watershed as a linear conduit, it makes obvious sense for both ecological and social management to develop a framework for ecosystem management within this sub-catchment context and provide the 'whole' catchment linkages in the successively broader scale, regional context in the hierarchy (Omernik and Griffith 1991, Cortner and Moote 1994, Griffith *et al.* 1994, Bryce and Clarke 1996, Allan *et al.* 1997, Omernik and Bailey 1997).

Catchment committees and community watershed initiatives provide an excellent forum for communication, information sharing, debating issues and mediation (Martin 1991). However, such efforts are rarely successful when undertaken at spatial scales too large to engage the interest or trust of community members. Using the appropriate spatial context would facilitate integration and coordination with the current system of management. It would assist stakeholders to identify and reach consensus on issues of common concern. This relates simply to the landscape setting (reflecting biophysical and topographical features) with which people identify and use. Communities living on the drier, inland tablelands where typical rangeland resource uses predominate (Bioregion X in Figure 9.1), have little in common with those living on the steep-faced coastal mountain ranges (Bioregion Y in Figure 9.1), or with people living along the coastal plains interested in intensive agriculture, marine based tourism and fisheries (Bioregion Z in Figure 9.1). Similarly, the numerous agencies with a mandate for water management throughout the catchment will also have different priorities and requirements that reflect the broader biophysical environment the catchment passes through (see Allan *et al.* 1997, Omernik and Bailey 1997).

An important part of most watershed management efforts is the monitoring of water quality. Many critics have raised concerns about the comparability of reference sites used for monitoring river basins and catchments (e.g., Omernik and Griffith 1991, Omernik and Bailey 1997, O'Neill *et al.* 1997). Monitoring of sediment loads, chemistry and biota down the length of the catchment provides only a snapshot of the river's features at any one time — data that are difficult to compare because of the variable influences of different landscapes the river flows through. These critics suggest that comparable and more meaningful monitoring data can be gathered by careful selection of similar monitoring sites across several streams within the same regional context. For example, Figure 9.1 indicates where reference sites (x, y, z) might be located across catchments within the same bioregional context (Bioregions X, Y, Z). Across the coastal marine interface, the influence of catchments on marine waters, sediment and nutrient transport and productivity across the continental shelf can be assessed (Figure 9.1, Bioregion Z; see also Chapter 7). The data from bioregional reference sites across catchments can also be integrated at larger and smaller hierarchical scales with other spatially attributed data (e.g., remote imagery) to collectively assess condition of vegetation, watershed and landscape ecosystem condition (Rollings 1996, O'Neill *et al.* 1997).

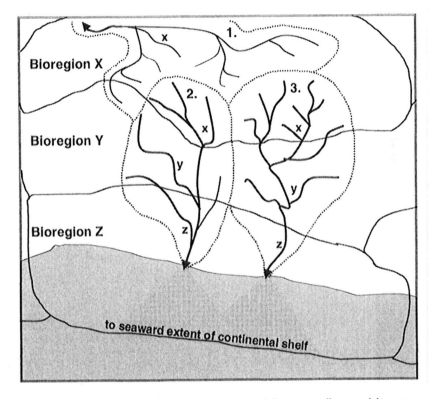

Figure 9.1. Three catchments (1-3) in the context of three generally typical bioregions representing the plateau rangelands (X), the coastal mountain ranges (Y) and, the coastal plain/inshore marine (Z). Monitoring data and reference sites (x, y, z) are best compared across catchments within the same bioregional context of biophysical elements, topography and land uses. See text for further explanation.

SUSTAINABLE MANAGEMENT WITHIN AND ACROSS BIOREGIONS

In contrast to the problems of watershed management, bioregions provide an appropriate context for application of catchment management principles. Greater management efficiencies and more meaningful monitoring for adaptive management can be gained through bioregional approaches to catchment management (Figure 9.1).

Paradigmatic shifts towards more holistic land and water management based on a landscape approach to ecosystem management are beginning to emerge, although the pace of change is slow (Cortner and Moote 1994, Lovejoy 1995). The integrative focus for efficient and effective ecosystem management, including application of catchment management principles should be the bioregion. Within a bioregional framework, monitoring linked to adaptive management provides direct feedback for action-based learning of the meaning of sustainability in that cultural, biophysical and land use context. Information and experience gained in the bioregional planning and management framework (reflecting nature and society at a local regional scale) will be more meaningful to local communities and institutions in developing new models for resource governance.

Bioregions are not isolated confines however — people, flora, fauna, water, air and goods and services flow between them. The nested hierarchy of bioregions within an ecoregional context, which in turn are part of larger continental and global ecological domains (see Chapter 2) provide successive frameworks which can guide policies and ecosystem management for a sustainable future.

CHAPTER 10

IMPLEMENTING A BIOREGIONAL FRAMEWORK

One way of looking at ... environmental history ... is to see the conflict between those who exploited the country to serve preconceived economic goals and imported attitudes of mind, and those on the other hand who sought to create a civilisation where human use of resources was compatible with a sense of identity with the land.

G.C. Bolton, 1981.

As we peer into the new millennium there appears an uncertain future, but with it a growing desire to regain an enduring balance between nature and society. A more focussed and applicable vision, however, must be cultivated to defeat the stubbornness and cynicism that halts much needed reforms in policy design and institutional function. The vision must engage our imagination and values, no matter what our politics might be. It must defy narrow definition and inflexibility while also elaborating a plan of action that can grow. It will need to revive the spirit of communities to balance the tide of globalisation, and facilitate civic engagement in building systems of environmental governance. Nonetheless, rapid change is unrealistic. Social and institutional change requires time for learning and adjustment; we have seen that an action-oriented approach to learning-by-doing might engage bottom-up, top-down and 'sideways-in' capacities along with the required transformations (Chapters 5 and 6).

Sustainability cannot be created and forced from afar. Ecologically oriented design for society's use and maintenance of natural resources and ecosystem services requires knowledge of place — the biocultural landscape on which we live and depend. Perhaps less romantic, but equally important is assessing our current status in that landscape region, including the social and governance institutions that influence the citizenry and effect ecological function (Berkes and Folke 1998, Brunckhorst 1998). In examining our ecological setting and developing a bioregional planning and management context, social and institutional change becomes possible — indeed, a part of the process.

In this chapter, I outline a general procedure that can assist development and implementation of an on-ground bioregional framework. Several operational steps are summarised, providing the basis for building towards a whole variety of alternative sustainable futures. It is not my intent to outline a strict prescription, such a formula would be impossible. Instead I offer a multi-national recipe, with a flexible list of ingredients, adaptable to the character of a region, its people and the shared knowledge of their landscapes (Figure 10.1).

Many of the ingredients necessary to bioregional planning are beginning to appear independently, both locally and nationally, in South-East Asia, Europe, Canada, USA, South America, Australia and Africa (examples are given in Chapter 6). This growing body of examples and case studies emphasises different aspects of assessment, planning, community participation and management. In each case, initial information is needed to understand landscape ecological structure and function, as well as sociological data on how people in the community and their present forms of governance view their environment (Figure 10.1).

BASIC ELEMENTS

There are three major elements in developing a bioregional framework for planning and ecologically sustainable development (Figures 10.1, 10.2).

The first element is to identify information needs and define a number of flexible, hierarchical management units. These will include multi-attribute biophysical regions, watershed or catchment components, ecological communities, agricultural and other natural resource use areas, and current land/sea tenure. All land management agencies, resource use representatives, local government and key individuals from the community must be involved.

The second element is to explore the various relationships between biophysical features and the perceptions local people have of 'their place.' This helps to identify bio-cultural landscapes (natural, semi-natural or modified) and to elucidate various options for bioregional frameworks. At this point, cultural mapping exercises can be a valuable tool (see Chapters

3, 5). Note again, that these are not strict ecological classifications or delineations but practical and flexible in terms of adapting social institutions towards 'broad-scale people management'.

The third major element in developing a bioregional framework is to allow a participatory process is to examine the implications of the outcomes from the first two elements (Figure 10.1).

KEY TASKS

What actions and consequences can be implied from the collected information and the various identified options in terms of planning and management for a sustainable future with communities and agencies as equal partners? These three elements involve several key tasks that will, and should, take time. Perhaps the key rule is to talk to lots of people. This process can be instigated by anyone in any position in the community. The work requires not only synthesising existing data about biophysical and social conditions, but also learning from the people in the region in order to identify their goals for a practical and realistic bioregional framework.

I will discuss six tasks that might be applicable in any country. These should be adaptable to a variety of situations, available data and tools; different communities will emphasise different parts of the process. Some activity will occur sequentially, some in parallel, and there will be times when apparently little is happening except thinking, adjustment and consensus building.

Multidisciplinary data collection and handling

Collection of data across a wide range of disciplines is a fundamental task. Focus will be on existing datasets, including quantitative and qualitative biophysical data and environmental surrogates for unknown data. No doubt, these data sets will need to be standardised to a spatial format in order to be integrated. Multiple attributes should be used, without any one having preferential weighting, to ensure the general applicability to a broad range of resource management issues (Chapter 2).

Understanding basic attributes of the landscape will be useful. These include existing plant and animal communities, surface and underling geology and soils, surface and underground hydrology, climate, physiography, and land use. Where data are scarce or missing, indicator species or ecosystems may be useful as surrogate information layers. Remote-sensed data, such as from NOAA, NDVI or AVHRR (Advanced Very High Resolution Radiometer), can give an indication of productive capacity through 'vegetation greenness' and vegetation classes, especially if mapped over several seasons and years. Ground-truthing surveys and finer scale

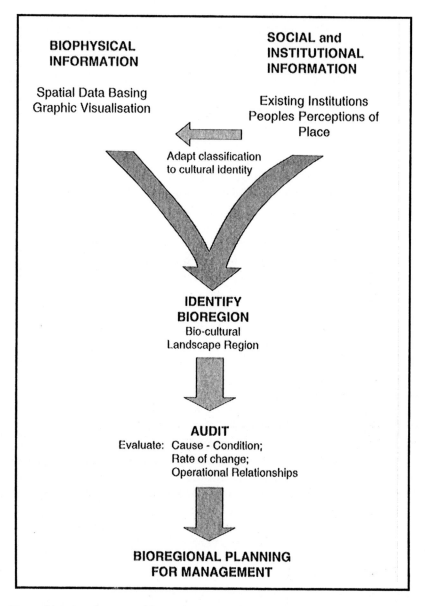

Figure 10.1. Initial steps and basic elements in the process of identifying a bioregional framework, which must be a pragmatic balance combining spatial assessment of biophysical and ecological functional elements with the social functional elements of the regional communities, participation and civic processes. Monitoring and adaptive, flexible management of the process itself will be necessary in building support and consensus.

data are always highly desirable, but not always possible. As new understanding evolves, an adaptive, iterative approach that allows updating of
information and adaptation of planning and management will be necessary.

It is highly desirable to develop data format standards, especially for
spatial data, including the means to assess or verify data where possible
and methods to analyse and synthesise relatively homogeneous regions
(see Wiken 1986, Omernik 1987, 1995, Thackway and Cresswell 1995,
Bailey 1996). Methods for data aggregation and display will be extremely
important for effective communication and to encourage feedback and
participative discussion within communities. GIS and other computer
visualisation techniques are increasingly proving valuable; however, simple
hand-drawn maps can do the job.

Gather and map community and social data

It is necessary to listen to lots of people and gather information from all
parts of the community (urban, rural, various sectoral interests etc) on
how people 'see' the landscapes in which they live and work. In order to
identify values across the community and discuss their relative importance, begin with a few questions such as:

- What do you and your community value about this area?
- What is special that you want to maintain?
- What needs fixing or special attention (social, environmental,
  economic)?
- Are these values local, regional or national in scope or significance?
- How might we better work together to sustain or develop community or
  civic directions suggested by these values?

Incorporation of all interests and understandings of the local landscapes
and their ecosystems will contribute to multiple uses of the final synthesis.
Indigenous understanding, use and management of the region and its
landscape ecosystems will be invaluable (e.g., Heinen 1995). Historical
records of settlement and early land use may also be useful. It will be
invaluable to spend time, not only gathering this information, but review-
ing it with local people. It will be most useful if this information can be
mapped, by hand or digitally on a GIS, in order to synthesise it with biophysical data and information about institutions such as government agencies and local government (next task below).

Inventory responsible agencies/jurisdictions

A comprehensive inventory of the many responsible agencies and government jurisdictions must be collated. It will be important, perhaps at the
outset, to develop partnerships with some of these agencies for information use, sharing and consensus planning. Spatial data on land tenure, census information and institutional jurisdictions will be needed. From this
information it will be possible to begin to identify the existing barriers to
collaboration, consensus building or integration for holistic management
across jurisdictions. Institutional mapping techniques and cultural mapping techniques may need to be developed (see Chapters 3, 4, 5).

Explore methods for trans-disciplinary synthesis.

Keep in mind always, that the data you collect will be used for multiple
purposes of decision-making, monitoring and assessment needs, not all of
which will be clear at the beginning. However, the first application of this
plethora of information and discussions will be to build a bioregional
framework for planning. Try various configurations (the framework will
have 'fuzzy' borders anyway) with citizens, community groups, resource
users, indigenous groups, agencies and local government (Figure 10.2).
Try an 'interim' experimental bioregion to start with, since it is likely to be
revised before being adopted. Plan plenty of time for review, communication and implementation of adaptations.

Examine integrative capacity of these institutions and existing processes.

Establishing an integrated management framework for cultural bioregions
will be a major step in moving from a cadastral to a bioregional approach
(Papadimitriou and Mairota 1996, Bunce et al. 1996). The pattern of management authority in the past has not always been a good fit when over-
layed onto a real landscape of interlaced structures and functions. A
bioregional framework allows the opportunity to compare the location of
existing management activity with the location of critical ecological and
social processes. Such a comparison will suggest ways to better align management with the living, changing landscape, and understand the consequences of particular activity. Reference sites and areas for broad scale
monitoring of natural resource quality will be important to measuring
integrity of the whole system, rather than just of small parts.

Encourage social and institutional transformations

Old models of agency jurisdictions over parts of the system will need to
give way to agency partnerships and shared responsibility for sustaining
the integrity of the whole system. Authority, as well as responsibility, will

devolve from large, central agencies to local land trusts where many partners are represented. Early engagement of local communities and agencies to identify their capacity for change will help to facilitate 'high ownership' of subsequent management actions through collaboration and consensus. Building local authority and responsibility will be a thoughtful, long-term activity, involving innovation and trust on the part of all participants (Chapter 5). Clear responsibility for specific implementation and management components need to be ascertained, assigned and monitored. The elaboration of new institutions or adaptation of existing ones should become possible through this process (Chapter 4). Always be prepared for compromise.

PLANNING FOR BIOREGIONAL MANAGEMENT

Following these initial tasks, it is possible to identify the bioregional framework for planning, as well as its components. The next stage in the process is to understand the condition of the bioregion by undertaking an environmental and social audit. Using information gathered earlier in the process, the audit evaluates causal relationships among all the components within the bioregion, noting the current condition and rates of change of key elements within the social and ecological system. During the initial scoping, it was important to ask, What is there? Now during the audit, we ask, How is it doing? and Where is it going?

This provides an opportunity to re-examine current land uses and existing protected areas in the new context of the identified bioregion (Figure 10.2). Potential new reserves can be assessed through explicit iterative reserve identification and selection procedures within bioregions, in order to ensure that protected area systems will collectively represent most elements of biodiversity. Iterative procedures allow maximum flexibility in the selection process — as several options may exist to achieve an explicit representation target and accomplish other ecosystem management objectives (Chapter 8). Alternative choices of national reserve networks can then be assessed against other goals such as viability, contiguity and land suitability.

Understanding the condition and trends of the social and ecological system will help to suggest places in the bioregion where current land uses are unsustainable, as well as assessing the bioregion's capacity for change toward a more sustainable future. Such an understanding can suggest several options for action. Nested in a hierarchy of social and ecological systems, the bioregional framework provides links through time and locality to help guard against negative impacts externalised to other places and generations (Chapter 9).

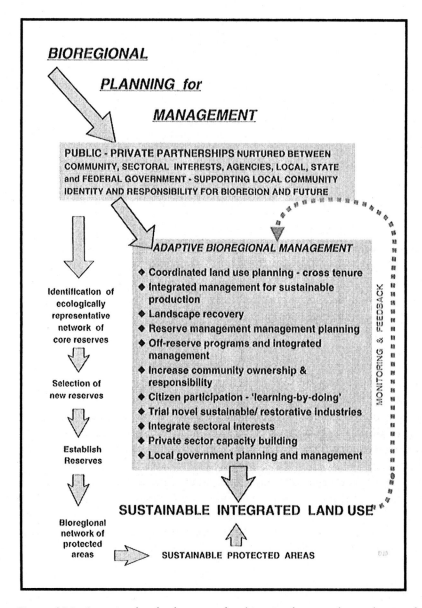

Figure 10.2. Steps in the development of a bioregional approach to planning for management. Identifying comprehensive and representative networks of protected areas, potential diversified resource use (including restoration) potential and, planning integrated land management within bioregions.

The bioregional framework provides a flexible framework for assessing the best solution to resolve cross-sectoral conflicts over land, river or sea use, as well as guidance for state and local government planning, and community group projects (Figure 10.2). For developing management strategies and effective feedback for flexible adaptation, this process builds on the elements mentioned above, but now in an action-oriented learning-by-doing program (Chapter 5). In order to use a bioregional framework for planning and decision-making, a successful strategy should:

- Become focussed on the process as much as the product;
- Be driven by the communities shared values and concerns;
- Be easily understood and encourage open communication;
- Be action oriented, but realistic;
- Provide long-term direction;
- Try to build consistency with other relevant strategies at State/National level; and
- Include a mechanism for on-going evaluation and feedback.

Successful management will depend on community participation carrying real responsibility, together with rules for resource use developed by the citizenry through some form of collective action. To ensure that resource users adhere to the rules for sustainability within the functional capacity of the bioregion, an enforcement capability will also be required that can be applied at various levels, from individual to agency (Chapters 4, 5).

Finally, a multi-layered system of adaptive management will be required (Chapters 7, 9). Bioregions will change, and monitoring must take place on a regular and on-going basis to measure trends in biodiversity, key ecological processes, human population growth, community attitudes and a variety of social, institutional, and economic attributes. The results should be fed back as adaptations to management or changes in organisational components (Figure 10.2).

In summary, this generalised procedure for developing and using a bioregional framework is designed to provide a flexible, iterative and adaptable (though scientifically based) tool-box for decision support and strategic planning. It provides tools for integrated management to deal with the following kinds of issues:

- Providing appropriate frameworks for natural resource assessment and monitoring.
- Integration across tenure or jurisdiction of land/sea resource planning, sustainable development and management.
- Identifying and trialing ecologically compatible, novel industries.

- Assisting adjustment of existing industries or production systems to better match ecological systems for long-term sustainability.
- Identifying reference sites for resource management (eg. water quality of comparable sub-catchments within the same bioregional context).
- Identifying bioregional networks of protected areas that maximise ecological representation and connectivity for ecological processes and flows; and, assist ecological monitoring.
- Providing an appropriate context for large-scale ecological restoration.
- Maximising information availability, access and decision support including a variety of visualisation techniques for multiple attributes at multiple scales (eg. GIS systems, remote sensing, Internet feedback to community and agency groups.
- Assessing the best options for resolving inter-sectoral conflicts over land-sea use,
- Facilitating public-private partnerships and other forms of decision-making capacity.
- Facilitating development of integrative natural resource policies at all levels of government.
- Guidance and decision support for integrative local government planning.
- Providing an appropriate (and comparable) context for State of the Environment reporting.
- Integration and coordination at a landscape scale to maximise efficiency of community group projects.
- Facilitating development of partnerships, community trusts, or commons to experimentally develop future land/sea management of common property resources, ecologically restorative industries.

CHAPTER 11

SUSTAINABLE FUTURES

This land is the place where we know where to find all that it provides for us — food from hunting and fishing, and farms, building and tool materials, medicines. This land keeps us together within its mountains: we come to understand that we are not just a few people or separate villages, but one people belonging to a homeland.

Akawaio Indian Chief, Upper Mazaruni District, Guyana (in Courrier ed., 1992)

The future is open to change. But what kind of future do we want? Clearly one that is healthy and sustained ecologically, socially and economically without imposing future costs on future generations. To actively pursue a sustainable future that will extend beyond the new millennium, we need to elaborate a vision owned by all sectors of local and regional communities. We then need to develop and implement various strategies to realise that vision within an appropriate spatial and temporal context. Good systems-based planning matches nature's functions with social functions to provide the objectives, strategies, actions and indicators to guide us towards a sustainable future and monitor our progress along the way. A bioregional framework can provide the required strategic context for action.

HUMAN SOCIETY AND THE BIOSPHERE

To achieve a sustainable society while maintaining biodiversity is one of the great challenges of our time. Sustaining ecological processes to support society's production needs and aspirations for quality of life would seem to be both utterly impossible and absolutely necessary. Add to this paradox the fact that nature is in retreat — under enormous pressure from human exploitation and population growth. The complex, entwined interdependence of all creatures and the products of these inter-relationships mean that ultimately human society is also threatened. Maintaining biodiversity and ecological processes is critically important to the future of human kind.

Decisive actions are needed. Cooperative, on-ground, public-private facilitated actions are required for a sustainable future. Such models are more likely to be successful if they are able to express the magnitude of social, cultural, economic and biological needs of society, and if they are based on the best available scientific understanding. (Gunderson *et al.* 1995, Stienitz *et al.* 1996, Holling and Meffe 1996, Brunckhorst 1998). This book outlines the tasks necessary for developing a framework for integrated planning and action toward a sustainable future. The bioregional approach expounded here is founded on principles of ecologically sustainable development coupled with restoration ecology, landscape ecology, and principles of ecosystem management.

OBSTACLES TO INTEGRATED PLANNING

Several obstacles limit the effectiveness of current approaches to integrated environmental planning and management. Contemporary planning and management paradigms commonly fail to produce information essential for coherent decision making, fail to meet socio-economic needs and, fail to conserve biological resources and ecosystem processes. Often, these failures relate more to lack of political determination and management problems than to lack of knowledge about ecosystems and human effects on them. Economic determinism, the decision model from Chapter 1, rationalises the waste of social and ecological resources for the greater good of the immediate economy. Narrowly focused institutional arrangements, excessive use of top-down approaches, and jurisdictional competition exacerbate the poor use of existing information. Such factors fragment decision making on multifaceted environmental problems. Recognition of the connectivity of nature (including human activity) across ecosystems suggests that even our attempts at 'ecosystem' management may be limited because of narrow application and traditionally compartmentalised institutional routines.

Public sector activity is essential but inadequate alone to effectively deal with the scale, complexity and inter-relatedness of environmental problems for long term sustainability (Chapter 4). Trans-disciplinary action including public sector partnerships with not-for-profit community groups and the private sector can be of great value in successful cooperative action and capacity building towards solutions. Australia's Strategy for Ecologically

Sustainable Development (agreed by all governments in 1992) recognises that partnerships between government and community at all levels is vital in the quest for integrated sustainable development and conservation.

PROTECTED AREAS — NECESSARY BUT NOT SUFFICIENT

Networks of protected areas provide one essential foundation for conservation of biodiversity; they are necessary, but utterly insufficient to do the job alone. The main objective of protected areas is to provide the foundation for maintenance of ecosystem function and biological diversity across landscapes and seascapes. A comprehensive reserve system is neither a panacea for securing ecological diversity, nor for sustainable resource use. Ultimately an adequate strategy depends on a variety of successful policies applied effectively outside reserves to ensure protection of landscape and seascape scale ecological functions, habitat restoration and ecologically sustainable use. A large proportion of biodiversity will always remain outside a reserve system. Therefore, networks of reserves must also be managed in concert with entire regions. Protected areas function as reference sites — essentially, they are measuring sticks for landscape-wide conservation and sustainability. So they are of value to local people who share responsibility for conservation across the landscape, both within and outside protected areas. Clearly, the quest for a sustainable future will be fought, and won or lost, across the various mosaics of human dominated 'cultural landscapes' where the vast bulk of biodiversity and ecological functional processes will always remain (Chapter 8).

In the past, establishment of protected areas has been neither scientific nor systematic. Selection of conservation reserves has usually been based on opportunism and/or *ad hoc* bureaucratic or political decision-making (Pressey 1994). Clearly such choices contribute little to maximising the conservation of biodiversity and, even less to maintaining ecological function across landscapes. They must not be allowed to limit future choices for sustaining dynamic ecosystems and functional processes. Most current systems of protected areas do not represent the diversity of ecosystems and species assemblages adequately. It is often unclear how individual reserves, large or small, contribute to the maintenance of ecological process and function at regional and larger scales. Therefore, future proposals for new reserves must be coherently selected and scientifically defensible. They should also aim to contribute to the social aspirations of users.

Through a variety of participative processes, discussed in earlier chapters, a bioregional approach has been developed for assessing and planning protected area networks and their management in context with the surrounding bioregion. It is also more important than ever to recognise that the functions of protected areas of all kinds, go far beyond the usual understanding of the word 'protection'. They are valuable, beyond their boundaries, in providing for the rehabilitation of environments, as nutrient sinks, for landscape stability and for the replenishment of species assemblages, or the protection of natural resource stocks for breeding or recruitment to other places. In highly modified and degraded areas, a principal objective of a protected area may be as much to restore ecosystems and their functions as to protect them. The role in habitat restoration and recombinant ecology for enlarging, redesigning and linking areas of critical ecological importance is also likely to become increasingly important for sustaining conservation and production areas.

LANDSCAPES, COMMUNITIES AND BIOREGIONS

Recognition of ecological and cultural linkages across landscapes is critically important in planning sustainable land use, establishing reserves and coordinating conservation efforts throughout the bioregion. Such linkages are obvious to us in nature; we need management systems that recognise our human links to natural processes and cultural realities. Thus, a bioregion is a similar and familiar group of landscape ecosystems. It is a region, made up of adjacent similar landscape ecosystems, with which local human communities identify because of how they see it, use it, and what it produces for them — whether mostly natural or modified to varying degrees (Chapter 3).

A bioregional planning framework helps achieve these linkages. Syntheses of scientifically credible and culturally meaningful characteristics are required in a bioregional planning framework to integrate ecological security with sustainable development objectives. Principles of landscape ecology link biodiversity, ecosystem function and wider landscape processes. The theory and experimental applications of the integrative framework provided by bioregions — similar adjacent, biocultural landscapes — based on landscape ecology is beginning to take shape.

A strategic bioregional framework for planning and management reflects nature and society, for it recognises the multi-stakeholder groups that are striving to establish cooperative programs to address ecological, cultural and economic issues at the scale of the regional landscape. If sustainability is to be an achievable human aspiration, barriers between fields of expertise must be minimised to encourage the capacity to understand the consequences of individual action on whole, integrated systems.

Scale is important. The bioregional scale described herein is the principal scale of human interaction with the environment; however human management in the environment is traditionally more narrowly focused. Size, shape, connectivity and distribution of social and ecological components are equally linked to multiple scales of biodiversity needs and human uses. The bioregional mosaic is logically made up of human communities having a particular identity with their own environment and its dynamic ecological processes. Each, naturally, has commonalties with neighbouring communities, towns and ecosystems in a shared bioregion. Community decision making for a sustainable future is therefore set in a context with the inter-relatedness of biological diversity and the connectivity of ecological functions and processes.

Community partnerships and strategic alliances with the private sector as well as government agencies can greatly increase the variety of resources and professional capacities that can be directed towards on-ground solutions. Such a broadly based, 'action centred', network of capacities can greatly contribute to an integrated, multi-disciplinary approach to conservation and sustainable development by empowering human communities to reach their potential in bioregional planning and management for a sustainable future.

There are four essential elements to facilitate effective community participation. First, efficient and sensitive communication networks between and within communities, participation by individuals and key stakeholder groups should be encouraged. Second, real responsibility for landscape scale (bioregional) land use planning should be given to the community and provision made for wide discussion of the implications of these responsibilities. Third, monitoring and direct feedback (adaptive management) are important steps in developing community ownership of decision making and innovative local solutions to environmental problems through 'learning-by-doing'. Finally, flexibility, self-regulation and self-empowerment are important ingredients to achieve conservation and sustainability goals. Possibilities and opportunities now abound where great difficulties exist — yet nature is not stagnant — so maximum flexibility is critical to successful bioregional planning and learning to live in a sustainable way (Smil 1993).

AN OPERATIONAL PLAN

In the previous chapter I have outlined an explicit course of action and steps for implementing bioregional planning, including development of a comprehensive and ecologically representative system of protected areas across a nation. The plan is not limited to application in federated countries such as Australia, Canada or the USA. Other countries could adopt such a process and implement the recommended course of action.

The plan is applicable across the biosphere. From a global-to-continental perspective, the identification of very broad-scale biophysical domains and ecoregions will help to foster inter-continental and international co-operation (Chapter 2). The strategy could then be implemented by any country wishing to develop a bioregional framework and assess conservation options for establishing representative networks of core reserves (IUCN category I or II protected areas) and, for planning complementary off-reserve land use and management. Brunckhorst *et al.* (1997) describe the first stage of implementation of this strategy in Australia.

At a general level, there are three tasks in developing bioregional frameworks. Initially, a multi-disciplinary team, preferably representing different jurisdictions (state, regional, local governments), should identify the information needs to define flexible, hierarchical management units such as continental ecoregions, bioregions, landscape ecosystems and patches (and as necessary for management, sub-catchments, species assemblages and structural units within the nested hierarchy; see Chapter 2). Logically and pragmatically, all existing data should be identified; on-going data collection and revision will always be necessary, but strategic implementation will be thwarted at this stage if the first decision is to 'wait for more research'. The next step requires the exploration of relationships between bioregions and peoples' perceptions of 'their place' — the cultural identity of communities with the environment and landscape in which they live. This leads on to the third step, which is to discuss the implications for assessment, planning and management with communities and agencies as equal partners (Chapter 11).

Identification of bioregions involves a pragmatic mixture of explicit biophysical regionalisation and readjustment according to the cultural identity of the communities that live there. The initial broad scale (hundreds of kilometres) biophysical regionalisation can be undertaken as a collaborative, cross-jurisdictional process to identify relatively homogenous environmental units. This environmental regionalisation should be followed by pragmatic adjustment of delineated regions to ensure cultural and community identity with the bioregion is affirmed — an essential requirement if bioregions are to be socio-politically useful tools for ecological sustainability goals.

Once developed, bioregional planning frameworks provide a unifying instrument for understanding dynamic ecological processes and social trends across landscapes. They can be valuable for developing community ownership and responsibility for resource management through public-private partnerships, facilitating institutional transformations, and experimentation with novel sustainable resource uses and productive sustainable land uses. They also provide a mechanism for coordinating ecological restoration, research and monitoring for adaptive management,

Bioregions are cultural landscapes for managing human activity. They provide an appropriate environmental context and scale in which to observe and monitor social transformations towards a sustainable culture. Development of indicators of both social and ecological carrying capacity will be essential for the assessment of the resilience of communities and bioregions to conditions or surprise changes that threaten quality of life. Such indicators might include, for example: population growth rates; natural resource consumption; pollution levels and rates of waste generation; air and water quality within and outside the region; ratios of natural areas to tar (roads and parking lots) or concrete (buildings, infrastructure); ecological productivity and quality; community and individual debt; employment, crime, health and welfare needs; and, level and quality of community participation in governance of the bioregion.

MOBILISING RESOURCES

The strength of national and community commitment to retaining biological diversity is clearly expressed by the effectiveness with which personnel and funds are mobilised for implementation of a conservation strategy. Detailed plans are essential, but the commitment of money and time are required for their realisation.

In many countries this seems a particularly difficult time to achieve increased funding for the environment. Governments in many countries are aiming to reduce budget deficits by reducing outlays and balancing the distribution of limited resources. They do not have all the funds required to implement the variety of programs and on-ground action to meet the challenges of environmental deterioration, biodiversity protection and sustainable resource use. On the other hand, difficulties in mobilising resources for environmental action also relate to societal perceptions of industrialisation, markets and economy. For example, the contemporary goal of economic 'growth' would seem to undermine efforts towards an economically and ecologically sustainable society. Therefore, concern for the environment must wait for flush times when the economics-dominated model suggests we can afford it.

Yet there are as well many signs which encourage realistic hope. Concern for the environment at the community level is growing in many countries, providing new, often widespread electoral potency. Conservation movements and green parties are only part of the map of political preference; the general population in many countries is more environmentally aware than ever before. Increasingly, governments are asked to demonstrate their attention to the environment — and so are corporations. As part of their public relations, private corporations often advertise their efforts to reduce pollution or protect nature. With shrinking government budgets, the contributions of the private sector are increasingly important in supporting integrated conservation action on the ground. Corporations, often demonised by conservationists for the sins of their industry, have become important partners in some cases, greatly enhancing the capacity for community-driven planning and action.

Non government, not-for-profit organisations are effective in mobilising support for the environment, and in many countries have made a major contribution to conserving threatened areas. By mustering and coordinating volunteers to assist with management they can be both effective and self-supporting. A little seed money from government or corporations can multiply their effectiveness and is a cost-effective use of scarce funds.

So there are many opportunities available to countries and communities to mobilise additional resources for maintaining biodiversity and securing continuing ecological functions. Community preferences suggest that there would commonly be electoral support for reallocating existing outlays from such activities as defence, intelligence services and programs for already relatively privileged groups towards environmental conservation. In some countries there has been sufficient support for a small increase in tax, particularly when the revenue is explicitly used for identifiable environmental programs.

The development of Bookmark Biosphere Reserve in South Australia illustrates many of these options for building the capacities of local communities to work towards a sustainable future within their own bioregional context. Located in an area of dry mallee adjacent to the Murray River, the region's long history of grazing and irrigation had left much of the upland exhausted and saline. Agriculture was in decline and communities along the river were beginning to feel the pinch of unemployment and an uncertain future. Throughout an area 300 kilometres across, there was little connection among the various landowners, lease holders, and patches of protected lands.

At about this time, a large pastoral lease became available on the fringe of the Australian Outback, and caught the attention of planners in Canberra. With financial help from the Chicago Zoological Society, the Australian government purchased the extensive lease, which linked the river communities to a protected National Park farther north, and the pieces for a regional scale Biosphere Reserve began to fall into place.

The idea of bioregional planning was new to the Riverland communities. How could the purchase of a huge, overgrazed chunk of mallee help them with their problems? The people in these communities were facing undeniable limits of their land's productivity. Yet when considered on a bioregional scale, they could see their connections to other communities, and to the condition of the larger landscape. Their problems were interconnected, and had to be tackled together. A bioregional framework connected the mallee, the floodplains, and the irrigation areas, and provided the context for people to work together toward planning a more sustainable future.

Community members met with agency and government representatives in sessions that sometimes lasted all night. The reserve offered the community a place to experiment with ecological restoration and new, compatible industry. The community offered the reserve a pool of local experience and knowledge as well as a dedicated volunteer force. Agency and government represent-atives offered the community the chance to identify their own goals, and helped develop a bioregional framework for meeting those goals.

Over the years, the bioregional identity has grown to include more leases, more communities, and more protected lands, coordinated by a trust committee of 13 members, of which most are local residents. New innovative industries are being tested to take advantage of the saline soils and find markets for the overabundance of grazing beasts in the mallee. River communities have begun ambitious restoration projects, attracting expertise and funds from groups interested in their efforts at ecologically sustainable development.

The Bookmark Biosphere Reserve is not unique. It is characteristic of a growing number of experiments around the world where bioregional frameworks are being developed to help communities plan for a sustainable future. Other, larger scale examples include the Mediterranean Blue Plan and the Great Lakes bi-national ecoregion. Ancient, enduring commons have shown us that it is possible to sustain the functions of nature and community through the changing course of a millennium. New relationships are now being forged between land and people that will be tested through the next millennium.

BIOREGIONS — SUSTAINABLE LANDSCAPES FOR A SUSTAINABLE FUTURE

So, how might nature and society be sustained through the unpredictable changes that will certainly occur in the future? In concluding, it is worth returning to this fundamental question. Clearly, securing the ongoing functional processes of ecosystems and landscapes is a necessary condition for securing human quality of life. Guaranteeing a good life for future generations is one of the key goals of social sustainability. Yet, if the choices of social institutions value sustained economic growth over ecological sustainability, then changing technology or amounting masses of data will be ineffective in halting our eventual destruction. The basic challenges have been clear for some time, yet most research and management has simply focused on small parts. There is still too little understanding of the relationship between society and ecosystems at the scale of regional landscapes — the bioregion.

The social system determines human objectives, and ecosystems provide a range of opportunities through which these objectives can be realised. So it should be possible to reconcile human needs and activities with maintenance of ecosystem function and sustainable land management, assembling bioregional frameworks for ongoing decision making about resource conservation and use. Farms, grazing areas, forests, and townships belong on the same planning grid as environmental recovery programs, endangered species restoration and protected areas. The scale of management of all activities must be tailored to both ecological processes and the needs of human communities. This is the strength of the bioregional planning approach.

This book describes a strategic approach for bioregional assessment and land use planning to sustain ecological function, and productivity for appropriate resource use within the limits of renewal. It is meant to be a flexible guide to help develop decision-making frameworks, identify representative reserve networks, and plan sustainable land uses within bioregions. We must ensure protected areas are sustainable and remain viable at broader, multiple spatial and temporal scales. We must ensure landscape-scale ecological restoration comes to be understood as a valuable and useful land use, as well as novel sustainable sequential land uses. We must build on social and cultural ties with landscapes to enhance institutional capacities and encourage new forms of resource governance. A bioregional framework provides a mechanism to integrate and coordinate planning for sustainable resource use and development, as well as for monitoring and feedback for adaptive management to ensure ecological security and a sustainable society.

Our common goal is the long-term sustainable future of nature and society beyond the new millennium; and into the following one. Can we do it? Any one of us can initiate the plan as a member of our community. Irrespective of position, we can facilitate the processes that bring together all the necessary institutional sectors, private and public capacities, and in partnership build the understanding necessary to pursue innovative bioregional assessment and planning for long-term, integrated resource management. The challenge remains with us all as individuals and as communities — each in our particular bioregional context — to persue a sustainable future with all vigour.

REFERENCES

Adinarayana, J., J.D. Flach and W.G. Collins, 1994. Mapping Land Use Patterns in a River Catchment Using Geographical Information Systems. *Journal of Environmental Management* 42: 55–61.

Albizuri, J.A. 1995a. The Urdaibai Biosphere Reserve: Conservation within a regional Development Perspective. *Biosphere Reserves Bulletin* 2: 12–14.

Albizuri, J.A. 1995b. The Urdaibai Biosphere Reserve. Paper Presented to UNESCO Conference on Biosphere Reserves, Seville, Spain, March, 1995.

Alexander, D. 1990. Bioregionalism: Science or Sensibility? *Environmental Ethics* 12: 161–173.

Allan, J.D., D.L. Erickson and J. Fay, 1997. The Influence of Catchment land Use on Stream Integrity across Multiple Spatial Scales. *Freshwater Biology* 37: 149–161.

Alpert, P., 1996. Integrated Conservation and Development Projects Examples from Africa. *BioScience* 46 (11): 845–855.

Argyris, C and D. Schon, 1978. *Organisational Learning*. London: Addison Wesley.

Armitage, D. 1995. An Integrative Methodological Framework for Sustainable Environmental Planning and Management. *Environmental Management* 19 (4): 469–479.

Bailey, R.G., 1976. Ecoregions of the United States map. US Department of Agriculture, Forest Service, Ogden, Utah, USA.

Bailey, R.G. 1996. Multi-scale Ecosystem Analysis. *Environmental Monitoring and Assessment* 39: 21–24.

Bailey, R.G., S.C. Zoltai, and E.B. Wiken, 1985. Ecological Regionalisation in Canada and the United States. *Geoforum* 16 (3): 265–275.

Barbier, E.B (ed), 1993. *Economics and Ecology: New Frontiers and Sustainable Development*. London: Chapman and Hall.

Barnsley, M.F., 1988. *Fractals Everywhere*. Boston: Academic Press.

Batisse, M. 1982. The Biosphere Reserve: A Tool for Environment Conservation and Management. *Environmental Conservation* 9(2): 101–111.

Batisse, M., 1990. Development and implementation of the biosphere reserve concept and its applicability to coastal regions. *Environmental Conservation* 17: 111–116.

Batisse, M., 1996. Biosphere Reserves and regional planning: a prospective vision. *Nature and Resources*. 32(3): 20–30

Belbin, L. 1993. Environmental Representativeness: Regional Partitioning and Reserve Selection. *Biological Conservation* 66: 223–230.

Bellah, R., R. Madsen, W.M. Sullivan [and others], 1991. *The Good Society*. New York: Alfred Knopf.

Berkes, F. and C. Folke (eds), 1998. *Linking Social and Ecological Systems: Management practices and Social Mechanisms for Building Resilience*. Cambridge: Cambridge University Press.

Bird, E. 1987. The social construction of nature: theoretical approaches to the history of environmental problems. *Environmental Review*, Winter 1987: 255–264

Black, A. and I. Reeve, 1993. Participation in landcare groups: the relative importance of attitudinal and situational factors. *Australian Journal of Environmental Management* 39: 51–57.

Botkin, D.B. 1992. Rethinking the Environment. *Dialogue* 16: 60–65.

Braatz, S., 1992. *Conserving Biological Diversity: A strategy for Protected Areas in the Asia-Pacific Region*. Washington D.C.: World Bank Technical Paper no. 193.

Bridgewater, P, A. Philips, M. Green and B. Amos, 1996. *Biosphere Reserves and the IUCN System of Protected Area Management Categories*. Canberra: IUCN, ANCA, UNESCO MAB.

Bromley, D.W. 1991. *Environment and Economy: Property Rights and Public Policy*. Oxford, UK: Basil Blackwell Ltd.

Bromley, D.W. 1992. *Making the Commons Work. Theory, Practice and Policy*. San Francisco: Institute for Contemporary Studies Press.

Brown, J. and MacLeod, N., 1996. Integrating Ecology into Natural Resource Management Policy. *Environmental Management* 20 (3): 289–296.

Brunckhorst, D.J. 1994. Protected Area Buzzwords — An Attempt to Define Some Current Terminology in a More Meaningful Way. 35–37 in Brunckhorst, D.J. (ed.) *Marine Protected Areas and Biosphere Reserves: 'Towards a New Paradigm'* Proceedings of the 1st International Workshop on Marine and Coastal Protected Areas, Canberra, Australia, August 1994. ANCA/UNESCO.

Brunckhorst, D.J., 1995. Sustaining Nature and Society — A Bioregional Approach. *Inhabit* 3: 5–9.

Brunckhorst, D.J., 1996. *A Strategy for Developing a Model Experimental Program for Landscape Recovery and Species Restoration on Bookmark Biosphere Reserve, the Riverland, South Australia*. Report Prepared for Bookmark Biosphere Trust, Dept. Environment and Natural Resources, South Australia, the Australian Nature Conservation Agency, and Chicago Zoological Society.

Brunckhorst, D.J. 1998a. Comment on 'Urban Governance in Relation to the Operation of Urban Services in Developing Countries' by Trudy Harpham and Kwasi A. Boateng. *Habitat International* 22 (1): 69–72.

Brunckhorst, D.J. 1998b. Creating Institutions to ensure sustainable use of resources. *Habitat International* 22 (3): 347–354.

Brunckhorst, D.J. and P. Bridgewater. 1994. A Novel Approach to Identify and Select Core Reserve Areas and to apply UNESCO Biosphere Reserve Principles to the Coastal Marine Realm. 12–17 in Brunckhorst, D.J. (Ed.) *Marine Protected Areas and Biosphere Reserves: Towards a New Paradigm*. Canberra: ANCA/UNESCO.

Brunckhorst, D.J. and P.B. Bridgewater, 1995a. Marine Bioregional Planning: A Strategic Framework for Identifying Marine Reserve Networks, and Planning Sustainable Use and Management, 105–116 in, N. Shackell and M. Willison (eds), *Marine Protected Areas and Sustainable Fisheries*. Proceedings 2nd Intl Conference on Science and the Management of Protected Areas, Halifax, Nova Scotia, 1994.

Brunckhorst, D.J. and P.B. Bridgewater. 1995b. Coastal Zone Conservation — Sustaining Nature and Society. 87–94 in, O. Bellwood, H. Choat and N. Saxena, eds, *Recent Advances in Marine Science and Technology '94*. PACON International and James Cook University

Brunckhorst, D.J., P. Bridgewater and P. Parker 1997. The UNESCO Biosphere Reserve Program Comes of Age: Learning by doing, landscape models for sustainable conservation and resource use. 176–182 in, P. Hale and D. Lamb (eds) *Conservation Outside Reserves*. University of Queensland Press.

Brunckhorst, D.J., J. Busby, S. Noble and W. Slater, 1994. *Managing Environmental Information on the Coastal Marine Realm*. State of the Marine Environment Technical Report. Canberra: AGPS: Commonwealth of Australia.

Brunckhorst, D.J., P. Coyne, I. Cresswell and R. Thackway. 1998 Australian Protected Areas — Toward a Representative System. *Journal of the Natural Areas Association* 18 (3): 255–261

Brunckhorst, D.J. and N.M. Rollings, 1999 Linking Ecological and Social Functions of Landscapes: I. Influencing Resource Governance. *Journal of the Natural Areas Association* 19 (1): 34–41.

Brussard, P.F., 1995. The President's Column — Critical Issues, *Society of Conservation Biology Newsletter, Vol 2 Issue1*.

Bryce, S.A. and Clarke, S.E. 1996. Landscape-Level Ecological Regions: Linking State-Level Ecoregion Frameworks with Stream Habitat Classifications. *Environmental Management* 20 (3): 297–311.

Bunce, R.G.H., C.J. Barr, M.K. Gillespie and D.C. Howard, 1996. The ITE Land Classification: Providing an Environmental Stratification of Great Britain. *Environmental Monitoring and Assessment* 39: 39–46.

Burnside, D.G. and S. Chamala. 1994. Ground based monitoring: A process of learning by doing. *Rangelands Journal* 16 (2): 221–237.

Caldwell, L.K., 1970. The Ecosystem as a Criterion for Public Land Policy. *Natural Resources Journal* 10 (2): 203–221.

Caldell, L.K. 1990. Landscape, law and public policy: Conditions for an ecological perspective. *Landscape Ecology* 5: 3–8

Carley, M and I. Christie, 1992. *Managing Sustainable Development*. London: Earthscan.

Castaneda, P.G.1993. Management Planning for the Palawan Biosphere Reserve, *Nature and Resources*. 29 (1–4): 79–82.

Chernyi, L. 1986. The Bioregional Vision – Far-sighted or Myopic? *Anarchy* 13: 7–12

Chester, S. and J. Rowley, 1992. Environmental Committees and Corporate Governance. *Company Director* 8 (10): 21–22.

Chua, T-E., 1993. Essential Elements of Integrated Coastal Management. *Ocean and Shoreline Management* 21: 81–108.

Church, R.L., Stoms, D.M. and Davis, F.W., 1996. Reserve Selection as a Maximal Covering Location Problem. *Biological Conservation* 7 (6): 105–112.

Clarke, S. E. and S.A. Bryce., 1999. Hierarchical subdivisions of the Columbia Plateau and Blue Mountains ecoregions of Oregon and Washington (level IV map of Oregon and Washington). *General Technical Report (GTR) 395*, US Forest Service, Pacific Northwest Research Station, Portland, Oregon.

Clarke, S.E., D. White, and A.S. Schaedel. 1991. Oregon, USA, Ecological Regions and Subregions for Water Quality Management. *Environmental Management* 15 (6): 847–856.

Coleman, W.G., 1996. Biodiversity and Industry Ecosystem Management. *Environmental Management* 20 (6): 815–825.

Commission for Environmental Cooperation, 1997. *Ecological Regions of North America*

(Level I and II maps). Commission for Environmental Cooperation (CEC). Montreal, Canada.

Commonwealth of Australia 1993. *Coastal Zone Inquiry: Final Report*. Resource Assessment Commission. Canberra: AGPS

Commonwealth of Australia 1996. *The National Strategy for the Conservation of Australia's Biological Diversity*. Canberra: Dept. Environment, Sport and Territories.

Commonwealth of Australia, 1996. *Australia: State of the Environment 1996*., Melbourne: CSIRO Publishing.

Cook, H.F. and C. Norman, 1996. Targeting Agri-environmental Policy: An Analysis Relating to the use of Geographical Information Systems. *Land Use Policy* 13 (3): 217–228.

Coop, P.C. and D.J.Brunckhorst, 1999. Triumph of the Commons: Age Old Lessons for Institutional Reform in the Rural Sector. *Australian Journal of Environmental Management* 6 (2): 23–30

Cortner, H.J. and M.A. Moote, 1994. Setting the Political Agenda: Paradigmatic Shifts in Land and Water Policy. 365–377 in Grumbine, R.E. (ed.), *Environmental Policy and Biodiversity*. Washington D.C.: Island Press.

Cortner, H.J. and M.A. Shannon, 1993. Embedding public participation in its political context. *Journal of Forestry* 91 (7): 14–16.

Costanza, R., 1993. Ecological Economic Systems Analysis: Order and Chaos. 27–45 in Barbier, E.B (ed), *Economics and Ecology: New Frontiers and Sustainable Development*. London: Chapman and Hall.

Costanza, R. and C. Folke, 1997. Valuing Ecosystem Services with Efficiency, Fairness and Sustainability as Goals. 49–68 in G.C. Daily (ed.), *Nature's Services: Societal Dependence on Natural Ecosystems*. Washington D.C.: Island Press.

Courrier, K. (ed.) 1992. *Global Biodiversity Strategy: Guidelines for Action to Save, Study and Use Earth's Biotic Wealth Sustainably and Equitably*. Washington D.C.: WRI, IUCN, UNEP.

Crance, C. and Draper, D., 1996. Socially Cooperative Choices: An Approach to Achieving Resource Sustainability in the Coastal Zone, *Environmental Management* 20 (3): 75–184.

Curtis, A. and T. De Lacy. 1994. *Landcare: does it make a difference?* Charles Sturt University: Johnston Centre for Parks, Recreation and Heritage 12: 1–79.

Dahlman, C.J. 1980. *The Open Field System and Beyond: A Property Rights Analysis of an Economic Institution*. Cambridge: Cambridge University Press.

Daily, G.C. (ed.) 1997. *Nature's Services: Societal Dependence on Natural Ecosystems*. Washington D.C.: Island Press.

Daly, H.E. and Cobb, J.B. 1989. *For the Common Good: Redirecting the Economy toward Community, the Environment, and a Sustainable Future*. Boston: Beacon Press.

De Leo, G.A. and S. Levin, 1997. The Multifaceted Aspects of Ecosystem Integrity. *Conservation Ecology* 1(1):3 URL:http://www.consecol.org/vol1/iss1/art3

di Castri, F., 1995. The Chair of Sustainable Development, *Nature and Resources* 31(3): 2–7.

Diamond, J.M., 1975. The Island Dilemma: Lessons of Modern Biogeographic Studies for the Design of Natural Preserves. *Biological Conservation* 7: 129–146.

DiSilvestro, R.L. 1993. *Reclaiming the Last Wild Places*. Wiley, New York.

Dovers, S.R., T.W. Norton and J.W. Handmer, 1996. Uncertainty, Ecology, Sustainability and Policy. *Biodiversity and Conservation* 5: 1143–1167.

Dutton, I.M., P. Saenger, T. Perry, G. Luker and G.L Worboys, 1994. An integrated approach to management of coastal aquatic resources — a case study from Jervis Bay, Australia. *Aquatic Conservation* 4 (1): 57–74.

Dutton, I. and P. Saenger, 1994. Expanding the Horizon(s) of Marine Conservation: The Challenge of Integrated Coastal Management. 18–27 in Brunckhorst, D.J. (Ed.) *Marine Protected Areas and Biosphere Reserves: Towards a New Paradigm*. Canberra: ANCA/UNESCO.

Dyer, M.I. and M.M. Holland 1991. The Biosphere Reserve Concept: The Need for a Network Design. *BioScience* 41(5): 319–325.

Ehrlich, P. R., 1995. Population and Environmental Destruction. 27–28 in A Report of the Senior Scientists' Panel, *Meeting the Challenges of Population, Environment and Resources: The Costs of Inaction*. Washington, D.C.: The World Bank.

Ehrlich, P.R. and A.H. Ehrlich 1992. The Value of Biodiversity. *Ambio* 21(3): 219–226.

Ehrlich, P.R. and E.O. Wilson 1991. Biodiversity Studies: Science and Policy. *Science* 253 (5021): 758–762.

ESA Ad Hoc Committee on Ecosystem Management, 1995. *The Scientific Basis for Ecosystem Management*. Pre-publication copy, Ecological Society of America, Washington D.C.

Fitzhardinge, G. 1994. An alternative understanding of the relationship between the ecosystem and the social system: Implications for land management in semi-arid Australia. *Rangelands Journal* 16 (2): 254–264.

Folke, C., Berkes, F, and Colding, J. 1998. Ecological practices and social mechanisms for building resilience and sustainability. In F. Berkes and C. Folke (eds). *Linking Social and Ecological Systems; Management Practices and Social Mechanisms for Building Resilience*. New York: Cambridge University Press.

Folke, C., Holling, C.S., and Perrings, C. 1996. Biological diversity, ecosystems and the human scale. *Ecological Applications*. 6 (4): 1018–1024

Foreman, D, J. Davis, D. Johns, R. Noss, and M. Soulé, 1992. The Wildlands Project Mission Statement. *Wild Earth* 1: 3–4.

Forey, P, C.J. Humphries, and R.I. Vane-Wright, 1994. *Systematics and Conservation Evaluation*. Oxford: Oxford University Press.

Forman, R.T.T., 1995. *Land Mosaics: The Ecology of Landscapes and Regions*. Cambridge: Cambridge University Press.

Forman, R.T. and M. Godron, 1981. Patches and structural components for landscape ecology. *BioScience* 31: 733–740.

Forman, R.T. and M. Godron, 1986. *Landscape Ecology*. New York: J. Wiley and Sons.

Francis, G., 1993. Ecosystem Management. *Natural Resources Journal* 33: 315–345.

Gardner, G.T. and Stern, P.C. 1996. *Environmental problems and human behaviour*. Allyn and Bacon. USA.

Gosz, J.R., 1995. Global Scale Networks for Ecological Research: Opportunities and Lessons Learned. Paper presented to UNESCO Conference on Biosphere Reserves, Seville, Spain, March, 1995.

Griffith, G.E., J.M. Omernik, T.E. Wilton, and S.M. Pierson, 1994. Ecoregions and Subregions of Iowa: A Framework for Water Quality Assessment and Management. *Journal of the Iowa Academy of Science* 10 (1): 5–13.

Grumbine, R.E. (ed.), 1994. *Environmental Policy and Biodiversity*. Washington D.C.: Island Press.

Grumbine, R.E., 1994. What is Ecosystem Management? *Conservation Biology* 8: 27–38.

Gubbay, S. and S. Welton, 1995. The Voluntary Approach to Conservation of Marine Areas. 199–227 in S.Gubbay (ed), *Marine Protected Areas: Principles and techniques for Management*. London: Chapman and Hall.

Gunderson, L., C.S. Holling and S. Light (eds), 1995. *Barriers and Bridges to the Renewal of Ecosystems and Institutions*. New York: Columbia University Press.

Haney, A and R. Power, 1996. Adaptive Management for Sound Ecosystem Management. *Environmental Management* 20 (6): 879–886.

Hanna, S., Folke, C. and Mäler, K.-G., 1996. *Rights to Nature: Ecological, Economoic, Cultural and Political principles of Institutions for the Environment*. Washington DC.: Island Press.

Hannigan, J.A. 1995. *Environmental Sociology: A Social Constructivism Perspective*. London and New York: Routledge.

Hansen, A.J. and di Castri F. (eds) 1992. *Landscape Boundaries: Consequences for Biotic Diversity and Ecological Flows.* Springer-Verlag, New York, Berlin. 439.

Hardin, G. 1968. The Tragedy of the Commons. *Science.* 162: 1243–1248.

Hastings, H.M. and G. Sugihara, 1993. *Fractals: A Users Guide for the Natural Sciences.* New York: Oxford University Press.

Hawken, P. 1993. *The Ecology of Commerce: How business can save the planet.* London: Weidenfeld and Nicolson.

Heinen, J.T., 1995. Application of Human Behavioural Ecology to Sustainable Wildlife Conservation and use Programmes in Developing Nations. *Oryx* 29 (3): 178–186.

Hempel, L.C. 1996. *Environmental Governance: The Global Challenge.* Washington DC.: Island Press.

Hine, D.W. and Gifford, R. 1996. Individual Restraint and Group Efficiency in Common Dilemas: The effects of two types of environmental uncertainty. *Journal of Applied Social Psychology* 26 (11): 993–1009

Hirvonen, H.E., L. Harding and J. Landucci, 1995. A National Marine Ecological Framework for Ecosystem Monitoring and State of the Environment Reporting. 117–129 in N. Shackell and M. Willison (eds), *Marine Protected Areas and Sustainable Fisheries.* Proceedings 2nd Intl Conference on Science and the Management of Protected Areas, Halifax, Nova Scotia, 1994.

Hobbs, R.J. 1993. Effects of Landscape Fragmentation on Ecosystem Processes in the Western Australian Wheatbelt. *Biological Conservation* 64: 193–201.

Hobbs, R.J. and S.E. Humphries, 1995.An Integrated Approach to the Ecology and Management of Plant Invasions. *Conservation Biology* 9 (4): 761–770.

Holling, C.S. 1986. The resilience of terrestrial ecosystems: local surprise and global change. In W.C. Clark and R.E. Munn (eds). *Sustainable Development of the Biosphere,* pp292–317, Cambridge University Press. Cambridge.

Holling, C.S and Meffe, M., 1996. Command and Control and the Pathology of Natural Resource Management, *Conservation Biology* 10 (2): 328–337.

Holling, C.S., Schindler, D.W., Walker, B.W. and Roughgarden, J. 1995. Biodiversity in the functioning of ecosystems: An ecological synthesis. 44–83 in, C Perrings, K.-G. Mäler, C. Folke, C.S. Hollong, and B.-O. Jansson (eds) *Biodiversity Loss: Economic and Ecological Issues.* Cambridge: Cambridge University Press..

Holmes, J.H. 1994. Changing values, goals, needs and expectations of rangeland users. *Rangelands Journal* 16 (2): 147–154.

Holmes, J.H. and P. Day, 1995. Identity, Lifestyle and Survival:Value orientation of South Australian Pastoralists. *Rangelands Journal* 17: 193–212.

Hooper, B.P. and J.A. Duggin, 1996. Ecological Riverine Floodplain Zoning:Its application to rural floodplain management in the Murray-Darling Basin. *Land Use Policy* 13 (2): 87–99.

Hooy, T. and G. Shaughnessy (eds) 1992. *Terrestrial and Marine protected Areas in Australia (1991).* Canberra: Australian National Parks and Wildlife Service.

HoRSCERA 1992. *Biodiversity: The Contribution of Community-Based Programs,* D.J.Brunckhorst (ed.), Report of the House of Representatives Standing Committee on Environment, Recreation and the Arts (HoRSCERA) Inquiry, Parliament of the Commonwealth of Australia. Canberra: AGPS.

HoRSCERA 1993. *Biodiversity: The Role of Protected Areas,* D.J.Brunckhorst (ed.), Report of the House of Representatives Standing Committee on Environment, Recreation and the Arts (HoRSCERA) Inquiry. Parliament of the Commonwealth of Australia. Canberra: AGPS

Hudson, W.E., (ed.), 1991. *Landscape Linkages and Biodiversity.* Washington D.C.: Defenders of Wildlife and Island Press

IUCN 1993. *Parks for Life.* Report of the IVth World Congress on National Parks and Protected Areas. IUCN, Gland, Switzerland.

IUCN 1994. Guidelines for Protected Area Management Categories. CNPPA with assistance of WCMC. IUCN, Gland Switzerland and Cambridge, UK. x, 261

Jensen, D.B., 1994. Conservation through Coordination: California's Experiment in Bioregional Councils. 273–279 in Grumbine, R.E. (ed.), *Environmental Policy and Biodiversity.* Washington D.C.: Island Press.

Johnson, K., F. Swanson, M. Herring and S. Greene, 1999. *Bioregional Assessments: Science at the Crossroads of Management and Policy.* Washington, D.C.: Island Press.

Kaus, A., 1993. Environmental Perceptions and Social Relations in the Mapini Biosphere Reserve. *Conservation Biology* 7 (2): 398–406.

Kaus, A., 1995. Linking Community and Conservation: Social Contracts in Mexico's Biosphere Reserve System. Paper presented to UNESCO Conference on Biosphere Reserves, Seville, Spain, March, 1995.

Kenchington, R. and G. Kelleher, 1995. Making a Management plan. 85–102 in S.Gubbay (ed), *Marine Protected Areas: Principles and techniques for Management.* London: Chapman and Hall.

Keohane, R. and E. Ostrom (eds), 1995. *Local Commons and Global Interdependence.* London: Sage.

Kiester, A.R., J.M. Scott, B. Csuti, R. Noss [and others], 1996. Conservation Prioritization using GAP Data, *Conservation Biology,* 10 (5): 1332–1342.

Kim, K.C. and R.D. Weaver (eds) 1994. *Biodiversity and Landscapes: a paradox of humanity.* New York: Cambridge University Press.

Kirkpatrick, J.B. 1983. An iterative method for establishing priorities for the selection of nature reserves: an example from Tasmania. *Biological Conservation* 25: 127–134.

Knudtson, P. and D. Suzuki, 1992. *Wisdom of the Elders.* Sydney: Allen and Unwin.

Lawrence, G. 1987. *Capitalism and the Countryside: The Rural Crisis in Australia.* Sydney: Pluto.

Leopold, A. 1949. A Sand County Almanac — And sketches here and there. New York: Oxford University Press (commemorative edition 1989).

Levine, B.L. 1986. The Tragedy of the Commons and the Comedy of Community: The Commons in History. *Journal of Community Psychology* 14: 81–99.

Li, Y., Y. Yan, Y. Yong. and Z. Chen, 1995. Xilingol Grassland Reserve: Role of Scientific Research in linking Nature Conservation with local Development. Paper presented to UNESCO Conference on Biosphere Reserves, Seville, Spain, March, 1995.

Lovejoy, T.E. 1995. Will expectedly the top blow off? Environmental trends and the need for critical decision making. *Bioscience Supplement- Science and Biodiversity Policy,* June 1995, 3–6.

Lowe, I. 1994. *Performance Measurement.* Proceedings of the 1994 Fenner Conference on the Environment, Canberra.

Ludwick, D., Hilborn, R. and Walters, C. 1993. Uncertainty, Resource Exploitation, and Conservation: Lessons from History. *Science* 260: 17–36.

Lusigi, W., 1984. Mt Kulal Biosphere Reserve: Reconciling Conservation with local human population needs. 459–469 in J. McNeely and D. Navid (eds), Conservation, Science and Society. Paris: UNESCO–UNEP.

Lyle, J.T., 1985. *Design for Human Ecosystems: Landscape, Land Use and Natural Resources.* New York: Van Nostrand Reinhold.

Maguire, L. 1994. Science, Values and Uncertainty: A Critique of the Wildlands Project. 267–272 in Grumbine, R.E. (ed.), *Environmental Policy and Biodiversity.* Washington D.C.: Island Press.

Maguire, L.A. and L.G.Boiney, 1994. Resolving Environmental Disputes: a Framework incorporating Decision Analysis and Dispute Resolution Techniques. *Journal of Environmental Management* 42: 31–48.

Margules, C.R., A.O. Nicholls and R.L. Pressey 1988. Selecting networks of reserves to maximise biological diversity. *Biological Conservation* 43: 63–76.

Margules, C.R., Cresswell, I.D. and Nicholls, A.O., 1994. A scientific basis for establishing networks of protected areas. In *Systematics and Conservation Evaluation.* (P. Forey, C.J. Humphries, and R.I. Vane-Wright Eds.), Oxford University Press.

Marshall, I.B., C.A.S. Smith and C.J. Selby, 1996. A National Framework for Monitoring on Environmental Sustainability in Canada. *Environmental Monitoring and Assessment* 39: 25–38.

Martin, P. 1991. 'Environmental Care in Agricultural Catchments: Toward the Communicative Catchment'. *Environmental Management* 15 (6): 773–783.

McBeth, M.K. and R.H. Foster, 1994. Rural Environmental Attitudes. *Environmental Management* 18: 401–411.

McHaug, I., 1969. *Design with Nature.* Garden City, N.Y.: Natural History Press.

McKean, M. 1992a. Success on the Commons: A comparative examination of institutions for common property resource management. *Journal of Theoretical Politics* 4 (3): 247–282.

McKean, M. 1992b. Management of Traditional Common Lands (Iriaichi) in Japan. 63–98 in, D.W. Bromley (ed) *Making the Commons Work: Theory, Practice and Policy.* San Francisco: Institute for Contempory Studies.

McKean, M. 1997. Common property Regimes: Moving from inside to outside. In B. J. McCay and B. Jones (eds), *Proceedings of the Workshop on Future Directions for Common Property Theory and Research.* New Brunswick, N.J.: Rutgers University; URL, http://www.indiana.edu/~iascp/webdoc.html

McLain, R.J. and R.G. Lee, 1996. Adaptive Management: Promises and Pitfalls. *Environmental Management* 20 (4): 437–448.

McNeely, J.A., 1988. *Economics and Biological Diversity: Developing and using Economic Incentives to Conserve Biological Resources.* Gland: IUCN.

Meidinger, E.E. 1997. Organizational and Legal Challenges for Ecosystem Management in K.A. Kohm and J.F. Franklin (eds) *Creating a Forestry for the 21st Century: The Science of Ecosystem Management.* Washington, D.C.: Island Press.

Meidinger, E.E. 1998. Laws and Institutions in Cross-Boundary Stewardship. 87–110, in R.L. Knight and P. B. Landres (eds) *Stewardship Across Boundaries,* Washington D.C.: Island Press.

Miller, D.H. 1978. The factor of scale: ecosystem, landscape mosaic and region. 63–88 in K. Hammond, G. Macinko andW.B. Fairchild (eds), *Sourcebook on the Environment: A Guide to the Literature.* Chicago: University of Chicago Press.

Miller, K.R., 1996. *Balancing the scales: Guidelines for increasing biodiversity's chances through bioregional management.* Washington D.C.: World Resources Institute.

Mumford, L. 1938. *The Culture of the Cities.* New York: Harcourt Brace.

Naeem, S., L.J. Thompson, S.P. Lawler, J.H. Lawton and R.M. Woodfin. 1994. Declining biodiversity can alter the performance of ecosystems. *Nature* 368: 734–736.

Nelson, J.G. and R. Serafin 1992. Assessing Biodiversity: A Human Ecological Approach. *Ambio* 21 (3): 212–218.

Ness, H. and E. Ezcurra, 1995. US-Mexico Biosphere Reserve Cooperation. Paper presented to UNESCO Conference on Biosphere Reserves, Seville, Spain, March, 1995.

Nicholls, A.O. and Margules C.R. 1993. An Upgraded Reserve Selection Algorithm. *Biological Conservation* 64: 165–169.

Norton, B.G. and R.E. Ulanowicz 1992. Scale and Biodiversity Policy: A Hierachical Approach. *Ambio* 21(3): 244–249.

Norton, T.W. and Dovers, S.R. 1996. Uncertainty, ecology, sustainability and policy, *Biodiversity and Conservation* 5: 1143–1167.

Noss, R.F. 1983. A Regional Landscape Approach to Maintain Diversity. *Bioscience* 33 (11): 700–706.

Noss, R.F. 1990. Can we maintain biological and ecological integrity? *Conservation Biology* 4: 241–243.

Noss, R.F. 1993. A Conservation Plan for the Oregon Coast Range: Some Preliminary Suggestions. *Natural Areas Journal* 13 (4): 276–290.

Noss, R.F. and A.Y. Cooperrider, 1994. *Saving natures Legacy: protecting and restoring biodiversity.* Washington D.C.: Island Press.

Noss, R 1992. The Wildlands Project Land Conservation Strategy. *Wild Earth* 1: 10–25.

Noss, R. 1994. The Wildlands Project: Land Conservation policy. 233–266 in Grumbine, R.E. (ed.), *Environmental Policy and Biodiversity.* Washington D.C.: Island Press.

Noss, R.F. and L.D. Harris, 1986. Nodes, Networks and MUMs: Preserving Diversity at all Scales. *Environmental Management* 10: 299–309.

O'Neill, R.V., C.T. Hunsaker, K.B. Jones, K.H. Riitters [and others], 1997. Monitoring Environmental Quality at the Landscape Scale: Using landscape indicators to assess biotic diversity, watershed integrity and landscape stability. *BioScience* 47 (8): 513–519

O'Neill, R.V., DeAngelis, D.L., Wade, J.B. and Allen T.F., 1986. *A Hierarchical Concept of Ecosystems.* New Jersey: Princeton University Press.

Odum, W.E. 1982. Environmental Degradation and the Tyranny of Small Decisions. *BioScience* 32: 728–729.

Omernik, J.M. 1987. Ecoregions of the conterminous United States (Level II). *Annals of the Association of American Geographers* 77 (1): 118–125 (and map supplement).

Omernik, J.M. 1995. Ecoregions: A spatial framework for environmental management. 49–62 in, W. Davis and T. Simon (eds), *Biological Assessment and Criteria: Tools for Water Resource Planning and Decision Making.* Boca Raton, Florida: Lewis Publishing.

Omernik, J.M. 1997. *Level III Ecoregions of the conterminous United States.* Published as a map. Corvallis, OR: US EPA.

Omernik, J.M. and Gallant, A.L. 1990. Ecoregions of the Upper Midwest States. US EPA Report no.600/3–88/037, US EPA Environmental Research Laboratory, Corvallis, Oregon.

Omernik, J.M. and Griffith, G.E. 1991. Ecological regions versus hydrologic units: Frameworks for managing water quality. *Journal of Soil and Water Conservation* 46: 334–340.

Omernik, J.M. and R.G. Bailey, 1997. Distinguishing between Watersheds and Ecoregions. *Journal of the American Water Resources Association* 33 (5): 1–15.

Omernik, J.M., S. Theile, C.Chapell, J. Kagan, T. Thorson and D. Paten, 1997. *Level IV Ecoregions of Oregon and Washington.* Published as a map. Corvallis, OR: US EPA.

Orr, D., 1992. *Ecological Literacy: Education and the Transition to a Postmodern World.* Albany: State University of New York Press.

Ostrom, E. 1990. *Governing the Commons. The Evolution of Institutions for Collective Action.* Cambridge: Cambridge University Press.

Palmer, M.A., J.D. Allan and C.A. Butman, 1996. Dispersal as a regional process affecting the local dynamics of marine and stream invertebrates. *Trends in Environment and Evolution* 11 (8): 322–326.

Papadimitriou, F. and P. Mairota, 1996. Spatial Scale-dependent Policy Planning for land Management in southern Europe. *Environmental Monitoring and Assessment* 39: 47–57.

Parsons, J.J. 1985. On 'bioregionalism' and 'watershed consciousness'. *The Professional Geographer* 37 (1): 1–10.

Pattee, H.H. 1973. *Hierarchy Theory: The Challenge of Complex Systems*. New York: Braziller.

Peccol, E., A.C. Bird and T.R. Brewer, 1997. GIS as a tool for assessing the influence of Countryside Designations and Planning Policies on Landscape Change. *Journal of Environmental Management* 47: 355–367.

Peterson, C.H. and J. Lubchenco, 1997. Marine Ecosystem Services. 177–194 in G.C. Daily (ed.), *Nature's Services: Societal Dependence on Natural Ecosystems*. Washington D.C.: Island Press.

Pipkin, J., 1996. Biological Diversity Conservation: A Public Policy Perspective. *Environmental Management* 20 (6): 793–797.

Platt, R.H., 1996. *Land Use and Society: Geography, Law and Public Policy*. Washington: Island Press.

Postel, S. and S. Carpenter, 1997. Freshwater Ecosystem Services. 195–214 in G.C. Daily (ed.), *Nature's Services: Societal Dependence on Natural Ecosystems*. Washington D.C.: Island Press.

Power, T.M., 1996. *Lost Landscapes and Failed Economies: The Search for a Value of Place*. Washington D.C.: Island Press.

Pressey, R.L. 1994. *Ad hoc* reservations: Forward or backward steps in developing representative reserve systems? *Conservation Biology* 8 (3): 662–668.

Pressey, R.L. and A.O. Nicholls 1989. Efficiency in Conservation Evaluation: Scoring versus Iterative Approaches. *Biological Conservation* 50: 199–218.

Pressey, R.L., C.J. Humphries, C.R. Margules, R.I. Vane-Wright and P.H. Williams 1993. Beyond Opportunism: Key Principles for Systematic Reserve Selection. *Trends in Ecology and Evolution* 8: 124–128.

Pressey, R.L., I.R. Johnson and P.D. Wilson 1994b. Shades of irreplaceability: towards a measure of the contribution of sites to a reservation goal. *Biodiversity and Conservation* 3: 242–262.

Pressey, R.L., M. Bedward and D.A. Keith 1994a. New procedures for reserve selection in New South Wales: maximising the chances of achieving a representative network. *Systematics and Conservation Evaluation* (P.L. Forey, C.J. Humpheries and R.I. Vane-Wright, eds), Systematics Association Special Volume 50: 351–362.

Price, A.R.C. and S.L. Humphrey, 1993. *Application of the Biosphere Reserve Concept to Coastal Marine Areas*: Papers Presented at the UNESCO/IUCN San Francisco Workshop, 14–20 August, 1989, Marine Conservation and Development Report, IUCN, Gland.

Ray, G.C. and B.P. Hayden 1992. Coastal Zone Ecotones. 403–420 in A.J. Hansen and F. di Castri (Eds), *Landscape Boundaries*, Springer-Verlag, Berlin.

Ray, G.C. 1991. Coastal Zone Biodiversity Patterns. *Bioscience* 41 (7): 490–498.

Ray, G.C. and M.G. McCormick-Ray, 1994. Coastal-Marine Protected Areas – A Moving Target. 2–9 in D.J. Brunckhorst (Ed.), *Marine Protected Areas and Biosphere Reserves: Towards a New Paradigm*. Canberra: ANCA/UNESCO.

Ray, G.C. and W.P. Gregg, 1991. Establishing Biosphere Reserves for Coastal Barrier Ecosystems. *BioScience* 41 (5): 301–309.

Ray, G.C., B.P. Hayden, A.J. Bulger and M.G. McCormick-Ray, 1992. Effects of global warming on the biodiversity of coastal-marine zones. 91–104 in R.L. Peters and T.E. Lovejoy (eds), *Global Warming and Biological Diversity*. New Haven: Yale University Press.

Rebelo, A.G. and W.R.Siegfried 1992. Where should Nature Reserves be Located in the Cape Floristic Region, South Africa? Models for Spatial Configuration of a Reserve Network Aimed at Maximising the Protection of Floral Diversity. *Conservation Biology* 6 (2): 243–252.

Reeve, I.J. 1992. Sustainable Agriculture: Problems, Prospects and Policies. 208–223 in Lawrence, G., Vanclay, F. and Furze, B. (eds.), *Agriculture, Environment and Society: Contemporary Issues for Australia*. Melbourne: MacMillan.

Reeve, I.J. 1997. Property and Participation: An Institutional Analysis of Rural Resource Management and Landcare in Australia. 83–95 in S. Lockie, and F. Vanclay (eds), *Critical Landcare*. Charles Sturt University, Australia: Centre for Rural Social Research.

Reeve, I.J. 1998. Commons and Coordination: Towards a Theory of Resource Governance. 54–65, in: Epps, R. (ed) *Sustaining Rural Systems in the Context of Global Change*. Proceedings of the Conference of the Joint IGU Commission for the Sustainability of Rural Systems and the Land Use — Cover Change Study Group, University of New England, Armidale, July, 1997. University of New England, Armidale.

Reid, T.S. and D.D. Murphy. 1995. Providing a Regional Context for Local Conservation Action: A natural community conservation plan for the southern California coastal sage scrub. *BioScience Supplement* 1995: 84–90.

Risser, P.G., 1995. Biodiversity and Ecosystem Function. *Conservation Biology* 9 (4): 742–746.

Rollings, N.M. 1996. Programming Task Orientated Image Processing Systems an Example for the Automated Land Cover and Land Use History Mapping from Satellite Imagery. In Zanetti and Brebbia (eds), *Development and Application of Computer Techniques to Environmental Studies VI*.

Rollings, N.M and D.J. Brunckhorst, (1999) Linking Ecological and Social Functions of Landscapes: II. Scale and Modelling of Spatial Influence. *Journal of the Natural Areas Association* 19 (1): 42–50.

Rolls, E. 1993. *From Forest to Sea*. Brisbane: University of Queensland Press.

Rowe, J.S., 1996. Land Classification and Ecosystem Classification. *Environmental Monitoring and Assessment* 39: 11–20.

Saberwal, V.K. and Kothari, A., 1996. The Human Dimension in Conservation Biology Curricula in Developing Countries, *Conservation Biology* 10 (5): 1328–1331.

Saetersdal, M., J.M. Line and H.J.B. Birks 1993. How to maximise Biological diversity and Nature Reserve Selection: Vascular Plants and Breeding Birds in Deciduous Woodlands, Western Norway. *Biological Conservation* 66: 131–138.

Sale, K., 1985. *Dwellers in the Land: The Bioregional Vision*. San Francisco: Sierra Club.

Samson, F.B., and F.L. Knopf, 1996. Putting "ecosystem" into natural resource management. *Journal of Soil and Water Conservation* (July–Aug. 1996): 288–292.

Saunders, D.A. 1990. The Landscape Approach to Conservation: Community involvement, the only Practical Solution. *Australian Zoologist* 26 (2): 49–53.

Schaaf, T. 1995. Sacred Groves: Environmental Conservation Based on Traditional Beliefs. *UNESCO Culture and Agriculture* 1995:43–45.

Schlager, E. and E. Ostrom, 1992. Property-rights Regimes and Natural Resources: a Conceptual Analysis. *Land Economics* 68 (3): 249–262

Schoonmaker, P.K., B. von Hagen and E.C. Wolf, (eds), 1997. *The Rain Forests of Home: Profile of a North American Bioregion*. Washington D.C.: Island Press.

Schoonmaker, P.K., B. von Hagen and E.L. Kellogg, 1997. A Vision for Conservation-Based Development in the Rain forests of Home. 383–406 in Schoonmaker, P.K., B. von Hagen and E.C. Wolf (eds), *The Rain Forests of Home: Profile of a North American Bioregion*. Washington D.C.: Island Press.

Schriever, J. and Birch, K., 1995. Implementing Ecosystem Management and Cumulative Effects Analysis on Oregon's Westside Forests. *GIS Symposium* 1995: 510–515.

Scott, J.M., B. Csuti, and S. Caicco, 1991. Gap Analysis: Assessing Protection Needs. 15–26 in Hudson (ed.), *Landscape Linkages and Biodiversity*. Washington D.C.: Defenders of Wildlife and Island Press

Scott, J.M., F. Davis, B. Csuti, R. Noss [and others], 1993. Gap Analysis: A Geographical Approach to Assessing Biological Diversity. *Wildlife Monographs* 123: 1–41.

Shannon, M.A., 1992. Community Governance: An Enduring Institution of Democracy. In, Congressional Research Service Senate Report, *Symposium on Multiple Use and Sustained Yield: Changing Philosophies for Federal Land Management*. Washington D.C.: Library of Congress.

Shannon, M.A., 1998. Understanding Social organizations and Institutions. 529–551 in, R.J. naiman and R.E. Bilby (eds), *River Ecology and Management: Lessons from the Pacific Coastal Ecoregion*. New York: Springer Verlag.

Slocombe, D.S. 1993. Implementing Ecosystem-based Management: Development of theory, practice and research for planning and managing a region. *BioScience* 43 (9): 612–622.

Smil, V. 1993. *Global Ecology: Environmental Change and Social Flexibility*. New York: Routledge.

Smith, H., C. Nagel, E.V. Gonzalez and M.H. Barajas, 1995. International Sonoran desert Alliance. Paper presented to UNESCO Conference on Biosphere Reserves, Seville, Spain, March, 1995.

Smyth, D. 1995. Caring for Sea Country – Accommodating Indigenous Peoples' Interests in Marine Protected Areas. 149–173 in S.Gubbay (ed), *Marine Protected Areas: Principles and techniques for Management*. London: Chapman and Hall.

Smythe, K.D., J.C. Bernabo, T.B. Carter and P.R. Jutro, 1996. Focusing Biodiversity research on the Needs of Decision Makers. *Environmental Management* 20 (6): 865–872.

Soulé, M.E. 1986. Conservation Biology and the Real World. 1–12 in, *Conservation Biology: The Science of Scarcity and Diversity* (M.E. Soule ed.). Sunderland, MA:Sinauer Associates.

Soulé, M.E. 1991. Conservation: Tactics for a Constant Crisis. *Science* 253 (5021): 744–750.

Soulé, M.E. 1992. A Vision for the Meantime. *Wild Earth* 1: 7–8

Soulé, M.E. and D. Simberloff 1986. What do genetics and Ecology Tell us About the Design of Nature Reserves? *Biological Conservation* 35: 19–40.

Soulé, M.E., ed., 1986. *Conservation Biology: The Science of Scarcity and Diversity*. Sunderland, MA: Sinauer Associates.

Soulé, M.E.,ed., 1987. *Viable Populations for Conservation*. U.K.: Cambridge University Press.

Spender, S. 1981. Poetry and the Modern City. 45–49 in M. Jaye and A. Watts (eds), *Literature and the Urban Experience*. Rutgers UP: New Brunswick, NJ.

Stanley, E.H., S.G. Fisher and N.B. Grimm, 1997. Ecosystem Expansion and Contraction in Streams. *BioScience* 47 (7): 427–435.

Stanley, M., 1983. The Mystery of the Commons: On the indispensability of civic rhetoric. *Social Research* 50 (4): 851–883.

Statzner, B., H. Capra, L.W. Higler and A.L. Roux, 1997 Focusing Environmental Management Budgets on Non-linear system Responses: Potential for Significant Improvement to freshwater Ecosystems. *Freshwater Biology* 37: 463–472

Steele, J.H. 1991. Marine Functional Diversity. *BioScience* 41 (7): 470–474.

Steinitz, C., 1993. A Framework for Theory and Practice in Landscape Planning. *GIS Europe*, July 1993: 42–45

Steinitz, C., M. Binford, P. Cote, S. Ervin [and others],1996. *Biodiversity and Landscape Planning: Alternative Futures for the Region of Camp Pendleton, California*. Harvard University, Cambridge, Massachesetts and U.S. Environmental Protection Agency. Report published by Harvard University Graduate School of Design for the Strategic Environmental Research Program, US DoD, US EPA, US DoE, DRI.

Strittholt, J.R. and R.E.J. Boerner, 1995. Applying Biodiversity Gap Analysis in a Regional Nature Reserve Design for the Edge of Appalachia, Ohio (U.S.A.), *Conservation Biology* 9 (5): 1492–1505.

Talbot, F. 1994. Coral Reef Protected Areas: What are they worth? 40–44 in Brunckhorst, D.J. (Ed.), *Marine Protected Areas and Biosphere Reserves: Towards a New Paradigm*. Canberra: ANCA/UNESCO.

Taylor, S.G. 1990. Naturalness: The concept and its application to Australian ecosystems. *Proceedings of the Ecological Society of Australia* 16: 411–418.

Thackway, R. and I. Cresswell (eds) 1995. *An Interim Biogeographic Regionalisation for Australia: A framework for establishing the national system of reserves.* Version 4.0, Canberra: Australian Nature Conservation Agency, Environment Australia.

Thackway, R. and I. Cresswell 1993. *Environmental Regionalisations of Australia: A user-oriented approach.* Canberra: Environmental Resources Information Network, Australian National Parks and Wildlife Service.

Thirsk, J., 1964. The Common Fields. *Past and Present* 29: 3–9

Thwaites, R. and T. Delacy, 1997. Linking Development and Conservation through Biosphere Reserves: Promoting Sustainable Grazing in Xilingol Biosphere Reserve, Inner Mongolia, China. 183–189 in, P. Hale and D. Lamb (eds) *Conservation Outside Reserves.* University of Queensland Press.

Thwaites, R., T. Delacy, B.Furze and Y. Li. 1995. Sustainable Development and Biodiversity Conservation in Xilingol Biosphere Reserve, China. Paper presented to UNESCO Conference on Biosphere Reserves, Seville, Spain, March, 1995.

Tisdell, C.A., 1995. Issues in Biodiversity Conservation including the Role of Local Communities. *Environmental Conservation* 22: 216–222, 228.

Tolba, M.K. and O.A. El-Kholy, 1992. *The World Environment, 1972–1992.* London: Chapman and Hall.

Tuchmann, E.T, K.P. Connaughton, L.E. Freedman, and C.B.Moriwaki, 1996. *The Northwest Forest Plan: A Report to President and Congress.* Portland, OR: U.S. Department of Agriculture, Office of Forestry and Economic Assistance, December, 1996.

U.S. Environmental Protection Agency. 1997. Level III ecoregions of the continental United States, Map M-1 (revision of Omernik, 1987). National Health and Environmental Effects Research Laboratory, Corvallis, Oregon.

Udall, S.L., 1988. *The Quiet Crisis and the Next Generation.* Salt Lake City, UT: Peregrine Smith.

UNESCO, 1995. The Seville Strategy for Biosphere Reserves. *Nature and Resources.* 31 (2): 2–17.

United Nations, 1983. *The Law of the Sea.* Official Text of the United Nations Convention on the Law of the Sea. Geneva

Urban, D.L., R.V. O'Neill and H.H. Shugart, Jr. 1987. Landscape Ecology: A hierarchical perspective can help scientists understand spatial patterns. *BioScience* 37 (2): 119–127.

Van Der Ryn, S and S. Cowan, 1996. *Ecological Design.* Washington, D.C.: Island Press.

Vane-Wright, R.I., C.J. Humphries and P.H. Williams, 1991. What to Protect? – Systematics and the Agony of Choice. *Biological Conservation* 55: 235–253.

Viles, H. and T.Spencer, 1995. *Coastal problems: Geomorphology, Ecology and Society at the Coast.* London: Edward Arnold / Hodder Headline

Walker, B. 1995. Conserving Biological Diversity through Ecosystem Resilience. *Conservation Biology* 9 (4): 747–752.

Walker, K.J. 1994, *The Political Economy of Environmental Policy: An Australian Introduction.* Sydney: University of New South Wales Press.

Walters, C.J. 1986. *Adaptive Management of Renewable Resources.* New York: Macmillan.

Walters, C.J. and Holling, C.S., 1990. Large-scale Management Experiments and Learning by Doing, *Ecology* 71 (6), 2060–2068.

Walton, D.W. and Bridgewater, P.B. 1996. Of Gardens and Garders. *Nature and Resources* 32 (3): 15–19.

Watson, J., 1993. Fostering community support for the Fitzgerald River Biosphere Reserve, Western Australia. *Nature and Resources* 29 (1–4): 24–28

Weeks, W.W., 1996. *Beyond the Ark: Tools for an Ecosystem Approach to Conservation.* Washington D.C.: Island Press.

Wells, S. and A.White, 1995. Involving the Community. 61–84 in S.Gubbay (ed), *Marine Protected Areas: Principles and techniques for Management.* London: Chapman and Hall.

Wescott, G.C. 1991. Australia's Distinctive National Parks System. *Environmental Conservation* 18 (4): 331–340.

Western, D., R. Wright and S. Strum (eds), 1994. *Natural Connections: Perspectives on Community-based Conservation.* Washington D.C.: Island Press.

Western, D. 1994. Ecosystem Conservation and Rural Development: The case of Amboseli. 15–54, in D. Western, R. Wright and S. Strum (eds), *Natural Connections: Perspectives on Community-based Conservation.* Washington D.C.: Island Press.

Western, D. and W. Henry, 1979. Economics and Conservation in Third World National Parks. *Bioscience* 29 (7): 414–418.

Wiken, E. 1986. Terrestrial ecozones of Canada. *Ecological land classification series* No. 19. Environment Canada, Ottawa, Ontario, Canada.

Wilson, E.O., 1992. *The Diversity of Life*, Penguin, London, New York.

Woinarski, J.C.Z., Price, O. and Faith, D.P., 1996. Application of a Taxon Priority System for Conservation Planning by selecting areas which are most distinct from environments already reserved, *Biological Conservation* 76: 147–159.

Young, M.D. 1992. *Sustainable Investment and Resource Use: Equity, Environmental Integrity and Efficiency.* Paris and Carnforth: UNESCO and Parthenon.

Young, O.R., 1995. The problem of sale in human/environment relationships. 27–45 in, R. Keohane and E. Ostrom (eds), *Local Commons and Global Interdependence.* London: Sage.

Zhao, X., 1995. *China's Biosphere Reserves.* Chineese national Committee for Man and the Biosphere programme. Beijing: Chen Guoanan (English issue).

INDEX